Library of
Davidson College

INDEX

INDEX

ABBREVIATIONS

AV	Authorized (King James) Version
BASOR	*Bulletin of the American Schools of Oriental Research*
BJRL	*Bulletin of the John Rylands Library* (Manchester)
CD	Covenant Document of Damascus (= Zadokite Work)
EQ	*Evangelical Quarterly*
E. T.	English translation
HTR	*Harvard Theological Review*
JBL	*Journal of Biblical Literature*
JRS	*Journal of Roman Studies*
LXX	Septuagint
MT	Massoretic Text
NTS	*New Testament Studies*
PTR	*Princeton Theological Review*
Q	Qumran
1QH	Thanksgiving (*Hōdāyōt*) Scroll from Qumran Cave 1
1QM	War (*Milḥāmāh* Scroll from Qumran Cave 1
1QpHab	Commentary (*pēsher*) on Habakkuk from Qumran Cave 1
1QSa	Rule of the Congregation (*Serek hāʿēdāh*) from Qumran Cave 1
4QpIsa[a]	First commentary on Isaiah from Qumran Cave 4
RSV	Revised Standard Version
SJT	*Scottish Journal of Theology*
TB	Babylonian Talmud
TDNT	*Theological Dictionary of the New Testament*, ed. G. Kittel and G. Friedrich, E. T. (Grand Rapids, Michigan)
ZNW	*Zeitschrift für die Neutestamentliche Wissenschaft*

not do violence to the original sense and context. These chapters present a pattern of revelation and response which the Evangelists recognize as recurring in the story of Jesus.

It is, I think, worthy of mention, as illustrating their sobriety and restraint, that none of them makes use of the utterance of Zechariah 13:6, where the man who tries to hide the fact that he is a prophet explains away the ecstatic wounds "between his hands" (RSV "on your back") by saying that he received them in the house of his friends. No New Testament writer tries to interpret this utterance as a prophecy of the nail-wounds in our Lord's hands, "in the grossest misapprehension of its meaning".[1]

There are obvious differences between the Evangelists' use of these six chapters of Zechariah and the use of scripture found in the Qumran commentaries. But in one important respect they have something in common; in neither community are events created to fit the scriptures – on the contrary, the scriptures are interpreted in the light of the events, although incidental details may be filled in from the prophecies. Parts of the passion narrative of the Gospels – especially the First and Fourth – are recorded in such a way as to present a commentary or *midrash* on Zechariah 9–14 and other prophetic scriptures, but that was because the Evangelists saw such a clear correspondence between the prophetic *testimonia* and the events to which the apostles and their associates testified as having taken place under Pontius Pilate.

---

[1] T. V. Moore, *The Book of Zechariah* (New York, 1856; reprinted, London, 1958), pp. 208 f.; it is astonishing that so able a Hebraist as E. B. Pusey should have been capable of this misinterpretation (*The Minor Prophets*, London, 1860, pp. 583 f.).

paschal lamb that suggested the story of the piercing to the Evangelist, he might almost be thought to have answered this argument in advance by the solemnity with which he assures his readers that these details were observed by an eyewitness whose reliability is beyond question.[1] As in other details of the passion story, it is the event that has suggested the *testimonium*, and not the other way about.

But in his brief reference to Zechariah 12:10 he has suggested something more than lies on the surface. The prophet compares the mourning over the pierced one to "the mourning for Hadad-rimmon in the plain of Megiddo"; but now the annually repeated lamentation for a fertility deity, never finished and always fruitless, has been swallowed up by the compassionate tears of penitent suppliants for a victim pierced once for all, never to be struck again. Moreover, whatever be the original reference of the piercing and the mourning,[2] in the passion narrative it has by implication been brought into close association with the oracle of Zechariah 13:7; the pierced one and the smitten shepherd are both recognized as pointing to Jesus, scourged and crucified as "the king of the Jews".

8. *Expulsion of Traders*

The cleansing of the temple in the Fourth Gospel is not closely bound up with the passion narrative as it is in the Synoptic Gospels; John, perhaps for programmatic reasons, places it at the beginning of the ministry, not at the end. But when he reports Jesus as saying, "you shall not make my Father's house a house of trade",[3] he may well be echoing the closing words of the book of Zechariah: "there shall no longer be a trader in the house of Yahweh of hosts on that day." The rendering "trader" (RSV) for "Canaanite" is at least as old as the Targum.[4] We might not have so readily seen an allusion to Zechariah 14:21b in this part of John's narrative were it not that we have such conclusive evidence elsewhere of his drawing upon Zechariah 9–14 as a source of *testimonia*.[5]

9. *The Argument from Prophecy*

If Jesus was the first to speak of His passion in terms of these chapters, the Evangelists follow His example not only in finding other foreshadowings of His passion there, but in finding them in a manner that does

---

[1] John 19:35.
[2] On Zech. 13:7-9 P. Lamarche says: "Ce morceau prolonge et explicite le passage qui lui est parallèle, 12: 10-13: 1" (*op. cit.*, p. 152).
[3] John 2:16.
[4] Targum on Zech. 14:21b, *taggarā* (cf. TB P^esāḥim 50a).
[5] In this context (2:17) John quotes from Psalm 69, another fertile source of messianic *testimonia* (cf. the quotation of the remainder of Psalm 69:9 in Rom. 15:3). Jesus' rebuke in Mark 11:17 points the contrast between "a house of prayer for all peoples" (Isa. 56:7) and "a den of robbers" (Jer. 7:11).

Whatever the historical occasion may have been, the wording of the oracle about the pierced one, like that of the oracle about the smitten shepherd, could conceivably be drawn from the national liturgy, and more particularly from the part played in that liturgy by the king.[1] It has even been suggested that the first person singular of the Massoretic text (". . . on *me* whom they have pierced") is taken verbatim from a royal utterance in the liturgy.[2] In our ignorance about the king's part in the liturgy we can at best note this as an interesting suggestion. In the context of the oracle the reading "on me" (if it is to be retained) would refer to Yahweh, who is the speaker, but it is not difficult to think of Yahweh as pierced in the person of His anointed representative.

The royal reference in the passage is underlined by the three-fold mention of the house of David.[3] The opinion that the pierced one is the Messiah is mentioned among others in the Palestinian Talmud; the Babylonian Talmud[4] ascribes to Rabbi Dosa (second century A.D.) the opinion that he is to be identified with Messiah ben Joseph, who falls in battle for his people in the war against Gog and Magog – an opinion later held by Rashi. But Messiah ben Joseph, conceived as a distinct personage from Messiah ben David, belongs to a later period than the apostolic age.

P. Lamarche compares the piercing of Yahweh's representative in Zecharaiah 12:10 with the piercing of the Suffering Servant in Isaiah 53:5.[5] He notes that two different Hebrew words are used, and that, so far as the language of Zechariah 12:10–13:1 is concerned, a closer parallel can be found with Ezekiel 36:25 f., where Yahweh promises that in the age of restoration He will purify Israel with clean water and put a new spirit within them. But he finds an association of *ideas* between the pierced one and the Suffering Servant, as also between the smitten shepherd and the Suffering Servant. Such an association may readily be found, and may best be explained if the pierced one, the smitten shepherd, and the Servant are all in their respective ways presentations of Israel's king enduring suffering and death in his people's place, thus procuring their cleansing, deliverance and peace with God.

The Fourth Evangelist's quotation of Zechariah 12:10, "they shall look on him whom they pierced", is not found in any other Gospel. There was of course, no occasion for another Evangelist to quote it, as John alone mentions the piercing of Jesus' side with the spear (as he is also the only Evangelist to make express reference to the nails by which Jesus' hands were pierced when He was crucified).[6] Should it be argued that it was this *testimonium* and the companion one from the directions for preparing the

---

[1] So F. F. Hvidberg, *Weeping and Laughter in the Old Testament*, E. T. (Leiden and Copenhagen, 1962), pp. 118 ff., followed by B. Otzen, *op. cit.*, p. 175.
[2] So F. F. Hvidberg, *op. cit.*, pp. 119 f., followed by B. Otzen, *op. cit.*, p. 180.
[3] Zech. 12:10, 12; 13:1.   [4] TB *Sukkah* 52a.
[5] P. Lamarche, *op. cit.*, p. 136.
[6] The nail-wounds may be implied in Luke 24:39.

they have pierced, they shall mourn for him, as one mourns for an only child, and weep bitterly over him, as one weeps over a first-born.

There is another reference to this passage in the Johannine literature of the New Testament, where the seer of Patmos announces Christ's coming with the clouds, when "every eye will see him, every one who pierced him, and all tribes of the earth will wail on account of him".[1]

The prophet goes on to describe the weeping in the following words:

> On that day the mourning in Jerusalem will be as great as the mourning for Hadad-rimmon in the plain of Megiddo. The land shall mourn, each family by itself; the family of the house of David by itself, and their wives by themselves; the family of the house of Nathan by itself, and their wives by themselves; the family of the house of Levi by itself, and their wives by themselves; the family of the Shimeites by itself, and their wives by themselves; and all the families that are left, each by itself, and their wives by themselves.
>
> On that day there shall be a fountain opened for the house of David and the inhabitants of Jerusalem to cleanse them from sin and uncleanness.[2]

While many suggestions have been made regarding the historical occasion of these words, Professor Eissfeldt sums the situation up by saying that "we cannot get further than confessing that we do not know, and that, so far as we can see, we are unlikely ever to know."[3]

Hadad-rimmon is a fertility deity, the one who sends rain to fructify the earth; the mourning for him was evidently a seasonal rite comparable to the mourning for Tammuz denounced by Ezekiel.[4] It may be that the mourning on his account was in due course historicized and reinterpreted as an annual lamentation for the death of good King Josiah, who fell in battle on that very plain of Megiddo. According to the Chronicler, "all the singing men and singing women have spoken of Josiah in their laments to this day" and this lamentation became "an ordinance in Israel"[5] – the same expression[6] as is used of the annual lamentation for Jephthah's daughter[7] (lamentation, like that for the pierced one, as "for an only child"), which also seems to be the historicization of an earlier fertility cult.

For long the mourning for Josiah was thought to provide our prophet's point of comparison for the mourning over the pierced one. As for the historical occasion of the piercing, a variety of views have been suggested – the assassination of the high priest Onias III in 171 B.C., for example, or of Simon the Hasmonaean in 134 B.C.[8] – but none of them carries conviction.

---

[1] Rev. 1:7. Cf. also Matt. 24:30, "and then all the tribes of the earth will mourn" (a non-Markan clause).
[2] Zech. 12:11–13:1.
[3] O. Eissfeldt, *The Old Testament: An Introduction*, E. T. (Oxford, 1965), p. 439.
[4] Ezek. 8:14.   [5] II Chron. 35:25.   [6] Heb. ḥōq beYiśrā'ēl.   [7] Judges 11:39 f.
[8] The former suggestion was E. Sellin's, the latter B. Duhm's (see O. Eissfeldt, *op. cit.*, p. 439).

but the son of perdition, that the scripture might be fulfilled".[1] This being so, it is not surprising that Matthew should find a further *testimonium* in Zechariah 11, where the services of Yahweh's shepherd are estimated at a mere thirty shekels.

It is worth observing, too, that Matthew evidently knows the variant "treasury" (Heb. *'ōṣār*) for "moulder" or "potter" (Heb. *yōṣēr*) in Zechariah 11:13 – a variant attested in the Peshitta and adopted by RSV. In his account it is almost as if the chief priests said: "How shall we fulfil this scripture? Shall we give it to the *'ōṣār* or to the *yōṣēr*? We cannot give it to the *'ōṣār* because it is blood money; let us give it to the *yōṣēr*."[2] So they bought the potter's field with it. They did not get the field, at any rate, out of the *testimonium*, and Matthew probably conflates this *testimonium* with another from Jeremiah, where a field is purchased. This, taken along with the story in Acts 1:18 f., rather suggests that a field was, as a matter of historical fact, bought with the reward of Judas's iniquity. I will not go farther, as one scholar invites us to do, and identify this field of Akeldama with the Qumran cemetery, purchased for a song to bury strangers in after the sediment of potter's clay had been worked out;[3] this calls for qualities of imaginative insight which I do not command.

7. The Pierced One

In John's passion narrative we are told how, just before sundown on Good Friday, the Roman soldiers broke the legs of the two men who were crucified on either side of Jesus, before removing their bodies from the crosses –

> but when they came to Jesus and saw that he was already dead, they did not break his legs. But one of the soldiers pierced his side with a spear, ... these things took place that the scripture might be fulfilled, "Not a bone of him shall be broken." And again another scripture says, "They shall look on him whom they have pierced".[4]

Of these two quotations, the former (from Exodus 12:46) marks Jesus out as the true Passover Lamb. The latter comes from Zechariah 12:10, where, after the defeat of the nations who take part in the end-time siege of Jerusalem, Yahweh says:

> And I will pour out on the house of David and the inhabitants of Jerusalem a spirit of compassion and supplication, so that, when they look on him whom

---

[1] John 17:12. A. Guilding (*The Fourth Gospel in Jewish Worship*, Oxford, 1960, p. 165) compares Zech. 10:10, LXX ("not even one of them shall be left behind").

[2] In any case, the "moulder" probably had his foundry in the temple treasury; cf. T. Reinach, *Jewish Coins*, ed. G. Hill (London, 1903), pp. 20–23: "once thrown into the Temple treasury, all gold and silver coins were melted down and transformed into ingots" (quoted by I. Abrahams, *Studies in Pharisaism and the Gospels*, series 1, Cambridge, 1917, p. 84).

[3] H. E. Del Medico, *The Riddle of the Scrolls*, E. T. (London, 1958), pp. 93 f.

[4] John 19:33–7.

into the treasury, since they are blood money." So they bought the potter's field with them, and that field, having been bought with blood money, came to be known as the Field of Blood. The Evangelist continues:

> Then was fulfilled what had been spoken by the prophet Jeremiah, saying, "And they took the thirty pieces of silver, the price of him on whom a price had been set by some of the sons of Israel, and they gave them for the potter's field, as the Lord directed me".[1]

The quotation is readily recognizable as coming from Zechariah 11:13, where the prophet tells what he did with the thirty shekels which his employers paid him for looking after their sheep.

> Then Yahweh said to me, "Cast it to the moulder – the lordly price at which I was paid off by them." So I took the thirty shekels of silver and cast them to the moulder in the house of Yahweh.

The Hebrew word ($y\bar{o}\underline{s}\bar{e}r$) translated "moulder" normally means "potter", but here it denotes the man who melted down precious metal in the temple mould or foundry.[2]

"There is", says Professor Dodd, "no reason to suppose that this [the incident of the thirty shekels] belongs to the primitive corpus of *testimonia*, but we may well believe that Matthew was led to it because the whole passage of Zechariah was already recognized as a source of testimonies."[3] Moreover, the belief that Judas's defection was a subject of Old Testament prediction is deeply embedded in the Gospel tradition. In Jesus' announcement of the betrayal in Mark 14:18-21, the words "The Son of Man goes as it is written of him, but woe to that man by whom the Son of man is betrayed!" may contain a hint that "that man" is also going as it is written of *him*. However that may be, the belief comes to full expression in Acts 1:10 ff., where Peter assures his fellow-disciples that "the scripture had to be fulfilled which the Holy Spirit spoke beforehand by the mouth of David, concerning Judas"; and goes on to quote two *testimonia* from the Psalter to show what he had in mind.[4] We remember too that in John's passion narrative Jesus applies to Judas the language of Psalm 41:9, "He who ate my bread has lifted his heel against me",[5] and later says in His prayer for His disciples, "none of them is lost

---

[1] Matt. 27:6-10. The reference to Jeremiah is usually explained as due to a testimony collection which conflated Zech. 11:13 with Jer. 18:2 f., where Jeremiah visits the potter's house, and Jer. 32:6-15, where Jeremiah buys the family field. R. H. Gundry thinks rather of a connection with Jer. 19:1-13, where the prophet, at the "Potsherd Gate", breaks a "potter's earthen flask" in token that Jerusalem will be destroyed like a "potter's vessel" and Topheth (the valley of the son of Hinnom) will become a burial place for its inhabitants "because there will be no place else to bury" (*The Use of the Old Testament in St. Matthew's Gospel*, Leiden, 1968, pp. 124 f.).
[2] LXX has $\chi\omega\nu\epsilon\upsilon\tau\acute{\eta}\rho\iota\omicron\nu$, "foundry".
[3] C. H. Dodd, *According to the Scriptures* (London, 1952), pp. 64 f.
[4] Psalms 69:26; 109:8.
[5] John 13:18.

several years ago by the late William Manson that this is probably not such a floating logion as some form critics have maintained. For, if Mark's setting is right, "this mountain" could only have been the Mount of Olives, which, according to Zechariah 14:4, was to be cleft asunder on the day when Yahweh came down to fight against Jerusalem's enemies. The natural inference is that not Mark but "*Jesus* had the Old Testament passage in mind, and the tradition followed by Mark was here true to history."[1] The logion is then a picturesque way of saying, "If only you have sufficient faith in God, the promised Day of the Lord will come more swiftly than you think."

The same passage of Zechariah, describing the siege and capture of Jerusalem, has influenced some of the language in the eschatological discourse, especially in its Lukan form, where the surrounding of Jerusalem with armies replaces the Markan allusion to the abomination of desolation.[2] And the flowing of living waters from Jerusalem, mentioned later in the same chapter of Zechariah,[3] may underlie the words of Jesus in John 7:38, spoken appropriately at the feast of Tabernacles: "as the scripture has said, 'from the midst thereof shall flow rivers of living water'".

There is in this interpretation of Zechariah 9-14 something quite different from the atomistic procedure which characterizes the Qumran commentaries on the Old Testament. One dominating principle – here, the portrayal of the shepherd-king – is discerned throughout the whole section of prophecy, and becomes determinative for the application of any part of it.

6. *Thirty Pieces of Silver*

With their Master's use of these chapters as a precedent, the Evangelists, as we might expect, had little difficulty in finding further correspondences between them and His ministry. In the "thirty shekels of silver" which were "weighed out" to the prophet for his services as shepherd of Yahweh's flock Matthew finds a *testimonium* for the money which the chief priests "weighed out" to Judas Iscariot for putting Jesus into their power;[4] his dependence on the Zechariah narrative (although he ascribes it to Jeremiah) becomes even plainer when he relates Judas's subsequent repentance, which is mentioned in none of the other Gospels. The chief priests, he says, took the thirty pieces of silver which Judas had thrown down before them in the temple, and said: "It is not lawful to put them

---

[1] W. Manson, *Jesus the Messiah* (London, 1943), pp. 29 f.
[2] Cf. C. H. Dodd, "The Fall of Jerusalem and the 'Abomination of Desolation'", *JRS* 37 (1947), pp. 47 ff.
[3] Zech. 14:8, based perhaps on Ezek. 47:1-12; cf. C. Mackay, "Zechariah in Relation to Ezekiel 40-48", *EQ* 40 (1968), pp. 197 ff.
[4] Matt. 26:15; cf. Zech. 11:12. It is perhaps a pity that RSV obscures the allusion by rendering ἔστησαν (so also in Zech. 11:12, LXX) "paid" instead of "weighed out"; for Matthew evidently departs from the wording of Mark 14:11 so as to conform to Zech. 11:12.

Say to the daughter of Zion
"Behold, your salvation comes...".

While the Old Testament passage is not quoted in the Markan account of the entry into Jerusalem (which is followed closely by Luke), it seems very probable that Jesus' decision to ride into Jerusalem on a colt[1] was understood as a fulfilment of Zechariah 9:9 even in the absence of an explicit quotation.

In the original context of the oracle there can be little doubt that the king who comes to Zion is the long-expected prince of the house of David.[2] We know how the rabbis of a later date debated this oracle: how could the Messiah come "meek and sitting on an ass" if he was also to come "with the clouds of heaven"? Rabbi Joshua ben Levi, who propounded the riddle, supplied his own solution: "If they are worthy, he will come with the clouds of heaven; if they are not worthy, meek and sitting on an ass."[3] But what was in the mind of Jesus as He carried out His plan to ride into Jerusalem thus? He certainly wished it to be known that He was presenting Himself to the city in that day of its visitation, not as a warrior-Messiah but as a peaceful prince – and indeed as Israel's shepherd-king, ready to "devote" himself for his people's salvation.[4] The attendant crowds who acclaimed "the coming kingdom of our father David"[5] grasped part of His intention, but they missed the more important part. We should take quite seriously the remark which the Fourth Evangelist appends to his quotation of Zechariah 9:9: "His disciples did not understand this at first; but when Jesus was glorified, then they remembered that this had been written of him and had been done by him."[6]

5. The Day of the Lord

In the light of this usage of Zechariah 9–14, other sayings and incidents in the Gospel narrative call for closer attention. The entry into Jerusalem was followed, a day or two later, by the incident of the unfruitful fig tree. In the context of this incident Mark places one of Jesus' sayings about faith: "Truly, I say to you, whoever says to this mountain, 'Be taken up and cast into the sea', and does not doubt in his heart, but believes that what he says will come to pass, it will be done for him."[7] It was pointed out

---

[1] W. Bauer's argument that πῶλος means "horse" except where it is evidently the young of a specified animal ("The 'Colt' of Palm Sunday", *JBL* 72, 1953, pp. 220 ff.) has been answered by O. Michel ("Eine philologische Frage zur Einzugsgeschichte", *NTS* 6, 1959–60, pp. 81 ff.) and H. W. Kuhn ("Das Reittier Jesu in der Einzugsgeschichte des Markusevangeliums", *ZNW* 50, 1959, pp. 82 ff.).
[2] See p. 75.
[3] TB *Sanhedrin* 98a. The implied identification of the Messiah with the "one like a son of man" who in Dan. 7:13 comes "with the clouds of heaven" is remarkable but not unparalleled in rabbinical tradition (cf. the messianic designation Bar Nafle, "son of the cloud", in *Sanhedrin* 96b; also the interpretation ascribed to Aqiba in TB *Ḥăgīgāh* 14a; *Sanhedrin* 38b).
[4] See p. 30.   [5] Mark 11:10.   [6] John 12:16.
[7] Mark 11:23.

in the Massoretic text (followed by AV and RV) "the poor of the flock" (*'ăniyyē haṣṣō'n*); RSV calls them "the traffickers in the sheep", following the Septuagint reading "Canaanites" and taking it to mean "traders" or "traffickers".[1] Whoever they may have been, they "were watching" the prophet as he annulled his "covenant" with the people by breaking his staff "Grace" and annulled the brotherhood between Judah and Israel by breaking its companion staff "Union". We have seen how "the poor of the flock" were interpreted in the *Zadokite Work* of the faithful community, and we may wonder whether Jesus' reference to His faithful followers as the "little flock" does not echo "the poor of the flock" in Zechariah 11:11 and "the little ones" against whom Yahweh's hand is turned in Zechariah 13:7. Whether there was an original connection between Zechariah 11:4–17 and 13:7–9 or not, Jesus at any rate draws on both passages in His self-portrayal as the repudiated and smitten shepherd.

4. *Behold, your king is coming!*

This being so, Jesus' entry into Jerusalem takes on a fresh significance. It is the two later Evangelists, Matthew and John, who expressly quote Zechariah 9:9 in this context.

Matthew says that He entered Jerusalem in this way "to fulfil what was spoken by the prophet, saying,

> 'Tell the daughter of Zion,
> Behold, your king is coming to you,
> humble, and mounted on an ass,
> and on a colt, the foal of an ass'."[2]

As is well known, Matthew separates the two parallel phrases at the end of the passage so as to see a reference to two animals instead of one, and the two animals appear in his actual narrative, as though to insist on the most literal fulfilment of the prophecy. John says that "Jesus found a young ass and sat upon it; as it is written,

> 'Fear not, daughter of Zion,
> behold, your king is coming,
> sitting on an ass's colt!'"[3]

These two quotations are independent of each other; they deviate both from the Massoretic Hebrew text, and from the Septuagint. John's quotation not only compresses the Zechariah text severely; it seems to conflate its opening words with Isaiah 40:9, as Matthew's rather fuller, but still abbreviated, quotation conflates them with Isaiah 62:11:

---

[1] The Massoretic and Septuagint readings are based on the same Hebrew consonantal text, variously divided: MT *kēn 'ăniyyē* ("thus the poor . . ."), LXX *kᵉna'ăniyyē* ("Canaanites", "traffickers").

[2] Matt. 21:4 f.   [3] John 12:14 f.

continued with Him in His trials,[1] that He had in mind when on the night of His betrayal He announced the fulfilment of the oracle "Awake, O sword". He Himself was the shepherd who was about to be struck; they were the sheep who were to be scattered. But beyond the striking and the scattering there was yet hope. "After I am raised up, I will lead you forth to Galilee."[2] The shepherd would come back to his scattered sheep, he would rally them again and continue to lead them as he had done in the past.

3. *The Thankless Flock*

When we see the quotation of Zechariah 13:7 not as something isolated, but as part of Jesus' presentation of Himself as the good shepherd, we begin to discern the germ of the use of Zechariah 9-14 in the Gospels, and especially in the passion narrative. For the figure of the shepherd recurs throughout these six chapters.

In Zechariah 9:16 those whom Yahweh delivers in the day of His intervention are "the flock of his people". In the following chapter His anger burns hot against the shepherds who have thus far ruled His people, "for Yahweh of hosts cares for his flock, the house of Judah".[3] In chapter 11 the prophet himself is commanded by Yahweh to serve as "shepherd of the flock doomed to slaughter",[4] because the existing shepherds exploit them and traffic in them. He obeys, and tends the sheep with his two staffs, named Grace and Union. By virtue of the authority divinely committed to him, he promptly deposes or destroys the unfaithful shepherds, three in number. But even so the sheep do not appreciate his services, and he becomes impatient with them. At last he refuses to be their shepherd any longer, breaks one of his staffs, and asks for his wages. He is paid thirty silver shekels, and he recognizes the insult implicit in this miserly sum – it was the price which, in the ancient covenant-law, a slave-owner received as compensation for a slave gored to death by someone else's ox.[5] But the prophet has been acting throughout as the agent and representative of Yahweh, the true Shepherd of Israel, and the insult is directed as much at Yahweh as at His servant. So, at Yahweh's command, this "lordly price" is appropriately disposed of, thrown into the temple foundry to be melted down, and the prophet breaks his other staff, betokening a dissolution of the national unity of all Israel.[6] The flock which has rejected a faithful shepherd receives once again a harsh and oppressive shepherd to take charge of it.

In much, though not all, of this passage (so hard to attach to a firm historical setting) Jesus saw His own rôle as the messianic shepherd foreshadowed. In the course of the passage reference is made to a group called

---
[1] Luke 22:28.   [2] Mark 14:28.   [3] Zech. 10:3.
[4] Zech. 11:4.   [5] Ex. 21:32.
[6] On the significance of the staffs and their breaking cf. B. Otzen, *op. cit.*, pp. 154 ff.

with reasonable certainty to be interpreted (in the Zadokite author's intention) of the Qumran community. They appear in another "shepherd" context in Zechariah 9–14, at which we shall look below, since it too has influenced the gospel story.[1]

There is, at any rate, no doubt about the application of the passage in Mark's passion narrative: the smitten shepherd is Jesus. Moreover, according to Mark, it is Jesus Himself who makes the identification. I have no doubt at all that Mark is right in ascribing this interpretation of the prophecy to Jesus; it is all of a piece with Jesus' presentation of Himself as the Shepherd of Israel – a presentation which can be traced in most of the Gospel strata.

On an earlier occasion in Mark's Gospel Jesus had compassion on a great throng of Israelites, "because they were like sheep without a shepherd".[2] As T. W. Manson used to point out, whereas we tend to think of this expression as though it meant "a congregation without a minister", here it should be understood rather in terms of its Old Testament usage, as in Micaiah ben Imlah's vision, where it means "an army without a general, a nation without a national leader".[3] It harks back to the picture of the shepherd-king.

The occasion when Jesus pitied the crowds who were leaderless and bewildered like sheep without a shepherd was just before the feeding of the five thousand. It is noteworthy that, in John's narrative, the crowds who had been fed tried to compel Jesus to be their king.[4] If He could supply their needs in the wilderness, could He not also lead them against their enemies? But Jesus did not let them have their way with Him. He was only too ready to be shepherd to the "lost sheep of the house of Israel",[5] but on His own terms, not on theirs. And when they realized that He was not going to be the kind of leader that they wanted Him to be, many of them refused to have Him as a leader at all, and gave up following Him.[6] The undesigned coincidences between the Johannine and Synoptic accounts of the feeding and its aftermath are too impressive to be dismissed as accidental, and we need not hesitate to make judicious use of details in the one account to illuminate details in the other.

The flock of Israel as a whole will not have Him as their shepherd, but there are some who persist in following Him, and with them He now makes a new beginning. By comparison with the nation, they are but a "little flock"; but in them lies the hope of the future. "Fear not, little flock", Jesus could say to them, "for it is your Father's good pleasure to give you the kingdom."[7] And it was the members of this little flock, who

---

[1] See pp. 105 f. [2] Mark 6:34.
[3] T. W. Manson, *The Servant-Messiah* (Cambridge, 1953), p. 70.
[4] John 6:15.
[5] A Matthaean expression (Matt. 10:6; 15:24).
[6] John 6:66. [7] Luke 12:32.

THE SHEPHERD KING 103

we may think, for example, of the annunciation formula of Isaiah's virgin oracle in the light of the much earlier Ugaritic poem, *The Wedding of Nikkal and Yarih*, with its introductory birth-announcement;[1] the reference in Micah 5:3 to "the time when she who is in travail has brought forth" probably shares the same kind of provenance. As for the "striking" of the king in the cultus, this may appear in a variety of oracles, notably in the third and fourth Servant Songs; perhaps also in the oracle of Micah where

> with a rod they strike upon the cheek
> the ruler of Israel.[2]

The "man who stands next to me" in the Zechariah oracle need not be regarded as a deliberate reference to the Suffering Servant, but if both he and the Servant are to be recognized as Israel's shepherd-king, the exegete may identify them even if the later of the two prophets did not.[3]

The oracle, "Awake, O sword, against my shepherd...", is quoted in one of the manuscripts of the *Zadokite Work*:

> But all the despisers of the commandments and ordinances [shall be visited with extinction] when God visits the earth to cause the recompense of the wicked to return upon them, when the word comes to pass which is written by the prophet Zechariah: "Awake, O sword, against my shepherd, against the man who stands next to me, says God; strike the shepherd, that the sheep may be scattered; I will turn my hand against the little ones." And those who "were watching" him are "the poor of the flock".[4]

It is difficult to be sure how the Zadokite author interpreted the smitten shepherd, because the quotation is thought to have been preceded by a lacuna in the archetype of the one manuscript which contains it; we may, with C. Rabin, think provisionally of the Teacher of Righteousness, though it would also be possible to argue that the Zadokite author had in view the judgement of a wicked ruler, the "worthless shepherd" of Zechariah 11:17.[5] But "the poor of the flock" who "were watching" are

---

[1] "A virgin will give birth... lo, a maid will bear a son" (lines 5, 7), where "virgin" and "maid" represent the Ugaritic equivalents of Heb. *bᵉtūlāh* and *'almāh* respectively (cf. C. H. Gordon, *Ugaritic Handbook*, Rome, 1947, p. 152; *Ugaritic Literature*, Rome, 1949, pp. 63 f.).

[2] Micah 5:1.

[3] P. Lamarche, *Zacharie IX-XIV* (Paris, 1961) has a section on "Relations littéraires entre Isaïe 40-55 et Zacharie 9-14" (pp. 131-47), in the course of which he concludes that "les rapprochements entre Zach 13, 7-9 et le Deutéro-Isaïe sont donc possibles, mais loin d'être certains" (pp. 137 f.).

[4] CD 19.5-9 (MS B).

[5] C. Rabin, *The Zadokite Documents*² (Oxford, 1956), p. 31 (he mentions a number of later Jewish interpretations of "the man who stands next to me"); F. F. Bruce, *Biblical Exegesis in the Qumran Texts* (London, 1960), p. 39. That a shepherd of another kind (one who would fleece the sheep) might be appointed over the people by way of punishment for their disobedience is implied also in Zech. 11:6, "I will cause men to fall each into the hand of his shepherd (so RSV, reading *rō'ēhū* for MT *rē'ēhū*, 'his neighbour'), and each into the hand of his king" (Heb. *malkō*, in which A. Guilding, *The Fourth Gospel and Jewish Worship*, Oxford, 1960, pp. 165 f., 232, unconvincingly finds the origin of the name Malchus in John 18:10).

Gethsemane on the night in which He was betrayed, "for it is written, 'I will strike the shepherd, and the sheep will be scattered'. But," He added, "after I am raised up, I will go before you to Galilee."[1] The last words are echoed in Mark's resurrection narrative: the young man who appears to the frightened women at the empty tomb says to them, "go, tell his disciples and Peter that he is going before you to Galilee; there you will see him, as he told you".[2]

The words "I will strike the shepherd, and the sheep will be scattered" are quoted by Jesus from an oracle in Zechariah 13:7-9:

> "Awake, O sword, against my shepherd,
>   against the man who stands next to me",
>   says Yahweh of hosts.
> "Strike the shepherd, that the sheep may be scattered;
>   I will turn my hand against the little ones. . . ."

The oracle goes on to tell how only a third of the population of the land will survive the impending time of trouble, when the sheep are scattered because their shepherd has been struck down, and even that third will undergo a fiery test as silver or gold is refined in the crucible. Then the ancient covenant terms will be confirmed afresh:

> They will call on my name
>   and I will answer them.
> I will say, "They are my people";
>   and they will say, "Yahweh is my God".[3]

The shepherd against whom the sword of Yahweh takes action can hardly be other than Israel's king. The motif of the scattering of the shepherdless sheep is a common one: its best-known Old Testament occurrence is Micaiah ben Imlah's prediction of Ahab's death at Ramoth-gilead: "I saw all Israel scattered upon the mountains as sheep that have no shepherd".[4] If there were any doubt about the royal status of the shepherd in Zechariah 13:7, it should be set at rest by Yahweh's further description of "my shepherd" as "the man who stands next to me",[5] for no man is so apt to be so described as Yahweh's anointed vicegerent, the king of Israel.

But which king of Israel? That this oracle did have a historical life-setting need not be doubted, but the present limitations of our knowledge prevent us from identifying it with any certainty. Whatever the historical life-setting was, however, the language of the oracle may well have a life-setting in the national cultus, in the liturgical rôle of the king.[6] The presence of such liturgical language in prophetic oracles is well enough established:

---

[1] Mark 14:27 f.   [2] Mark 16:7.
[3] Is this the blood-sealed covenant of Zech. 9:11?   [4] I Kings 22:17.
[5] Heb. *geber 'ămîtî*; cf. "the man of thy right hand" (Psalm 80:17).
[6] Cf. B. Otzen, *Studien über Deuterosacharja* (Copenhagen, 1964), pp. 192-4; he includes a liturgical and eschatological with a historical interpretation – Zedekiah in 587 B.C.

> He shall stand and feed his flock in the strength of Yahweh,
>   in the majesty of the name of Yahweh his God,
> And they shall dwell secure, for now he shall be great
>   to the ends of the earth.[1]

Yahweh Himself is the supreme "Shepherd of Israel" who leads His people "like a flock";[2] Moses, David and all the others to whom the task of governing His people is entrusted are under-shepherds, responsible to Him. The coming Messiah of David's line is depicted in more than one of Ezekiel's oracles as the good shepherd, in welcome contrast to a succession of unworthy shepherds who enriched themselves at the expense of the flock;[3] reference has already been made to one of these oracles as the background of the parable of the shepherd and the sheep in John 10.[4] But there is another group of Old Testament oracles which may have influenced Jesus' thinking on this subject more profoundly than that of Ezekiel: those contained in the last six chapters of the book of Zechariah. These chapters are included by C. H. Dodd among the "primary sources of testimonies" used by the primitive church;[5] according to R. C. Dentan, they "had an extraordinary significance for the early Christian community.... Some scholars believe that the influence of this material upon the formation of the gospel tradition was even more pervasive than a mere list of quotations would indicate."[6]

There are no more vexed problems in Old Testament criticism than the life-setting of Zechariah 9–14. These chapters comprise two groups of oracles, each of which (like the following book of "Malachi") begins with the words "An oracle: the word of Yahweh";[7] but the historical contexts of the units contained in these two short corpora can only be guessed at. Dates ranging from the closing phase of the Hebrew monarchy to the early Hasmonaean period have been suggested.[8] It is always open to us to hope that some new discovery will lighten our darkness. In spite of lively expectations cherished when the Qumran texts were first discovered, they have not supplied the desired light. Here, however, we are concerned rather with the influence of these chapters on the New Testament, and especially on the passion narratives.

2. The Smitten Shepherd and the Scattered Sheep

"You will all fall away", said Jesus to His disciples as He led them out to

---

[1] Micah 5:4. [2] Psalm 80:1; cf. Psalm 23; Isa. 40:11.
[3] Ezek. 34:23 f.; 37:24; cf. Jer. 23:1–6; Ps. Sol. 17:45 (where the coming Messiah is pictured as "shepherding the flock of the Lord faithfully and righteously").
[4] See p. 80.
[5] C. H. Dodd, *According to the Scriptures* (London, 1952), p. 107 (cf. also pp. 64–7).
[6] R. C. Dentan, "Zechariah", *The Interpreter's Bible* vi (New York, 1956), p. 1089.
[7] Zech. 9:1; 12:1; cf. Mal. 1:1.
[8] See O. Eissfeldt, *The Old Testament: An Introduction*, E. T. (Oxford, 1965), pp. 434–40; B. Otzen, *Studien über Deuterosacharja* (Copenhagen, 1964), pp. 11–34.

CHAPTER VIII

THE SHEPHERD KING

"The good shepherd lays down his life for the sheep."

1. The Shepherd of Israel

THE PORTRAYAL OF THE IDEAL KING AS A SHEPHERD IS COMMON FORM IN ancient Near Eastern literature and farther afield too. Egypt and Greece, among other areas, provide ready parallels to the biblical material.[1] In the Old Testament not only is the relation between a ruler and his subjects repeatedly expressed in terms of a shepherd and his sheep; two of the greatest leaders of Israel in Old Testament history, Moses and David, served their apprenticeship by keeping sheep – a fact which might prompt a course of meditation on the characteristics shared in common by sheep and human beings, which call for similar qualities of leadership

> Thou didst lead thy people like a flock
> by the hand of Moses and Aaron[2]

is the witness of an Asaphite psalmist, while a prophet refers to the same occasion in the question:

> Where is he who brought up from the sea
> the shepherd of his flock?[3]

Whether the shepherd is singular or plural, whether the reference is to a human leader or leaders or to Yahweh Himself as "the Shepherd of his flock", the Septuagint rendering (which corresponds with the translation given above) is the basis on which the writer to the Hebrews speaks of "the God of peace who brought again from the dead our Lord Jesus, the great shepherd of the sheep, by the blood of the eternal covenant".[4] The Sea of Reeds has become the nether abyss,[5] from which the Saviour has returned to reign as the Shepherd-King.

In Micah's Bethlehem oracle it is said of the coming "ruler in Israel":

---

[1] In Egypt (c. 2000 B.C.) the sage Ipuwer describes the ideal king as "the herdsman of all men" who "has spent the day caring for them" (tr. J. A. Wilson in *Ancient Near Eastern Texts Relating to the Old Testament*[2], ed. J. B. Pritchard, Princeton, 1955, pp. 441 f.). As for Greece cf. the regular Homeric description of Agamemnon as "shepherd of the hosts (peoples)" (Ἀγαμέμνονα ποιμένα λαῶν, *Iliad* ii. 243, etc.). See J. Jeremias in *TDNT* vi, pp. 486 f.
[2] Psalm 77:20.   [3] Isa. 63:11.
[4] Heb. 13:20.   [5] Cf. Rom. 10:7.

Professor C. K. Barrett a few years ago.[1] It is good for assumptions to be sceptically examined, but I remain persuaded that this saying declares Jesus' own understanding of His mission, and an understanding of it in the spirit of the Servant who offers up his life as a reparation for others and bears the sin of many. The concept of death as an atonement for sin is familiar in Judaism: the criminal about to be executed is instructed to pray, "May my death atone for all my sins",[2] while "the death of the righteous makes atonement" for others.[3] The men of Qumran regarded their toil and tribulation as procuring atonement for the land and the godly martyrs under Antiochus willingly yielded up their lives as a propitiation to avert the divine wrath from their nation: "through them the nation obtained peace".[4] The men of Qumran and the martyred *ḥasīdīm* under Antiochus are to be closely associated with the *maśkīlīm* of Daniel, who in turn are modelled on the Servant of Yahweh. But Jesus goes back to the fountain-head and appeals to what was *written*. Not that His saving work was a matter of painstakingly consulting and reproducing a programme written down in advance; He transcended the letter of prophecy while fulfilling its spirit in giving His life as "a ransom for many". This phrase "for many" recurs in the words of institution over the cup at the last supper, "my covenant blood which is poured out for many"[5] – the variant phrase "for you" found in the Pauline account and the longer Lukan account of the institution[6] is probably a liturgical adaptation emphasizing the personal relevance of the cup and the covenant. The event, in any case, has shown that "many" who have appropriated this relevance have experienced the atoning virtue of the obedience and death of Christ – on a scale (as was announced in reference to the Servant) incomparably greater than the atoning virtue effected by those other martyr-deaths. We conclude that, in the words of Professor H. H. Rowley:

> there is no real reason to deny that Jesus believed that His death would be unique in its effect, with a uniqueness which could only be expressed in terms of the Suffering Servant, and that in objective, historical fact His belief has been justified.[7]

[1] C. K. Barrett, "The Background of Mark 10:45", in *New Testament Essays*, ed. A. J. B. Higgins (Manchester, 1959), pp. 1 ff. For a more general critique see M. D. Hooker, *Jesus and the Servant* (London, 1959).
[2] Mishnah, *Sanhedrin* 6.2.   [3] *Leviticus Rabba* 20.7
[4] 4 Maccabees 18:4 (see p. 29 with n. 10).
[5] Mark 14:24.
[6] I Cor. 11:25; Luke 22:20 (see p. 54 with n. 2).
[7] H. H. Rowley, *From Moses to Qumran* (London, 1963), p. 26.

In the development of the gospel tradition we discern a tendency towards the increasing ascription to Him of the phrase "Son of Man" in place of the pronoun "I";[1] but this tendency arose from the fact that "Son of Man" was already recognized as a distinctive usage of His.

(b) The suffering of the Son of Man may be *implied* by the earlier literature in which the designation occurs, even by Daniel's account of "one like a son of man", but it was not explicitly stated there. The evidence that Jesus introduced a new and unwelcome idea to His disciples when He told them that the Son of Man must suffer cannot so easily be treated as an explanation after the event of their disillusionment at His death: Peter's expostulation with Him for talking like that and His sharp rebuke of Peter have the "ring of truth" about them.[2]

(c) Jesus' repeated insistence that the suffering of the Son of Man was a subject of Holy Writ, up to the time when He submitted to His captors with the words "Let the scriptures be fulfilled",[3] cannot satisfactorily be set down in its entirety to the reflection of the early church on the coincidence of promise and fulfilment. Moreover, it demands something more than the possible implication that Daniel's "one like a son of man" is a suffering figure. If Jesus, as the men of Qumran appear to have done, brought together the figures of the Servant of Yahweh and the Son of Man and gave them a unitive interpretation, He was probably reproducing the originally intended identification of the Son of Man with the Servant. The scriptures that must be fulfilled need not be looked for outside the Hebrew Bible; and within the Hebrew Bible no passage has such strong claims for consideration as the fourth Servant Song. The Son of Man's vocation to "suffer many things and be rejected", attested in the Markan and non-Markan traditions in divergent Greek wording which may represent variant renderings of a Semitic original,[4] must precede his glorious advent as truly as the humiliation and death of the Servant precede his elevation; and this vocation is something that is "written" concerning him.

(d) "The Son of Man also came not to be served but to serve, and to give his life as a ransom for many"[5] is the utterance which, above all others ascribed to Jesus in the Gospels, sums up His mission in the spirit of the fourth Servant Song. The generally assumed dependence of the saying on the language of the Song was subjected to critical and salutary scrutiny by

---

[1] Compare Mark 8:27 ("Who do men say that I am?") with Matt. 16:13 ("Who do men say that the Son of Man is?").

[2] Mark 8:31-3.

[3] Mark 14:49. See p. 29 above.

[4] Mark 8:31; 9:12; Luke 17:25 (see p. 28 above). The "rejection" emphasis may come from Psalm 118:22 (see p. 65), where LXX has ἀποδοκιμάζω (the verb used in Mark 8:31; Luke 17:25); the verb ἐξουδενέω in Mark 9:12 (cf. ἐξουθενέω in the quotation in Acts 4:11) is perhaps influenced by a Greek version of Isa. 53:3, where Aquila, Theodotion and Symmachus all translate Heb. *nibzeh* (RSV "despised") by ἐξουδενωμένος. Cf. B. Lindars, *New Testament Apologetic* (London, 1961), pp. 81, 169 ff.

[5] Mark 10:45.

not to Jesus Himself? Professor Dodd's words about the basic principle of Old Testament interpretation in the New may be applied with special emphasis to this particular instance:

> To account for the beginning of this most original and fruitful process of re-thinking the Old Testament we found need to postulate a creative mind. The Gospels offer us one. Are we compelled to reject the offer?[1]

Jesus did more for His followers than the Teacher of Righteousness did for the men of Qumran, but the lines of biblical exegesis which characterize the literature of the one community and the other are best traced back to their respective founders.

There was, no doubt, a natural transition of thought from the words which follow "Behold my servant" at the beginning of the first Servant Song (addressed to Jesus by the heavenly voice at His baptism) to those which follow "Behold my servant" at the beginning of the fourth Song, but we should not assume that Jesus in fact made this transition and drew the practical conclusions from it if we did not find evidence of the influence of the fourth Song in His thinking and speech. This evidence is present in most of our Gospel strata; it is interwoven in large measure with the evidence for His use of the expression "Son of Man" about which something was said in an earlier chapter.

This is not the occasion to enter in detail into the arguments involved in coming to terms with the Evangelists' ascription of this expression to Jesus as a self-designation.[2] Let me state four propositions, each of which invites controversy which must be engaged in elsewhere:

(a) Jesus spoke of Himself as the "Son of Man".
(b) He spoke of the "suffering" Son of Man.
(c) He spoke of the Son of Man's suffering as something which was "written".
(d) He spoke of the Son of Man's suffering as "a ransom for many".

(a) The fact that the New Testament places the expression "Son of Man" on the lips of Jesus and not of His followers (with the single significant exception of Stephen)[3] is as plain a pointer in one direction as the fact that the expression "Son of David" is used of Him by His followers and not by Himself is in another direction; the setting of the "Son of Man" is in the ministry of Jesus, not in the life and thought of the primitive church.

---

[1] C. H. Dodd, *According to the Scriptures* (London, 1952), p. 110. In particular, he "can see no reasonable ground" for doubting that Jesus "associated with the Son of Man language which had been used of the Servant of the Lord, and employed it to hint at the meaning, and the issue, of His own approaching death" (*ibid.*). Cf. R. T. France, "The Servant of the Lord in the Teaching of Jesus", *Tyndale Bulletin* 19 (1968), pp. 26 ff.

[2] See works by F. H. Borsch, A. J. B. Higgins, H. E. Tödt and M. D. Hooker mentioned on p. 26, n. 5, p. 28, nn. 2, 4; also A. J. B. Higgins, "Son of Man-*Forschung* since 'The Teaching of Jesus'", in *New Testament Essays: Studies in Memory of T. W. Manson*, ed. A. J. B. Higgins (Manchester, 1959), pp. 119 ff.; M. Black, "The Son of Man in Recent Research and Debate", *BJRL* 45 (1962-63), pp. 305 ff.

[3] Acts 7:56, to be related to the promise of Luke 12:8 (see p. 28).

sake God made him to be sin"¹ (i.e. a sin-offering, as in Isaiah 53:10);² "Jesus our Lord... was put to death for our trespasses";³ God is described as "sending his own Son in the likeness of sinful flesh and as a sin-offering".⁴ The hymn reproduced in Phil. 2:5–11 celebrates the humiliation and exaltation of Jesus as the Servant-Messiah, although the bearing of sin is not mentioned in it.⁵ Jesus' bearing of sin is, however, emphasized in language borrowed from the fourth Servant Song in Hebrews (Christ was "offered once to bear the sins of many")⁶ and I Peter; the latter document, indeed, draws freely on this Song to depict the patient submission of Jesus under unjust suffering, in which He left an example for His followers to imitate, and amplifies the statement that the Servant "bore the sin of many" to declare that Jesus "himself bore our sins in his body on the tree, that we might die to sin and live to righteousness."⁷

In the Apocalypse the identity of the suffering Servant with the conquering Messiah is portrayed when the "Lion of the tribe of Judah" appears in the presence of God, fresh from the scene of his victory, in the guise of "a Lamb standing as though it had been slain" – a figure in which we may see combined the paschal lamb "without blemish or spot" and the Servant of Yahweh "like a lamb that is led to the slaughter".⁸ The Messiah triumphed through suffering and death, and His followers must tread the same path: this is the lesson of the Apocalypse.⁹

The same combination of the paschal lamb with the lamb led to the slaughter of Isaiah 53:7 probably underlies the description of Jesus in the Fourth Gospel as "the Lamb of God, who takes away the sin of the world".¹⁰ It is a matter of additional interest that in Palestine Aramaic the word *ṭalyā* (quoted in its feminine form in Mark 5:41) could mean "lamb" "servant" or "child" as the context might require;¹¹ but apart from this we have here a clear application to Jesus of the sin-bearing and sin-removing ministry of the Servant.

5. *Jesus and the Servant*

The interpretation of the achievement of Jesus in terms of the obedience of the suffering Servant is so widely spread in the New Testament as to create a presumption that it goes back behind them all, and to whom i

---

¹ II Cor. 5:21; the following clause, "so that in him we might become the righteousness of God" echoes the sense of Isa. 53:11.
² In Isa. 53:10 the Septuagint renders Heb. *'āshām* (see p. 87, n. 6) by περὶ ἁμαρτίας "sin-offering").
³ Rom. 4:25; "put to death" is literally "delivered up" (παρεδόθη, as in Isa. 53:12, LXX)
⁴ Rom. 8:3.   ⁵ See p. 82, nn. 1, 2.   ⁶ Heb. 9:28.
⁷ I Peter 2:24.   ⁸ Rev. 5:5. See pp. 79 f. above.   ⁹ Rev. 12:11.
¹⁰ John 1:29 (cf. 1:35). His taking away sin is reminiscent of Isa. 53:12.
¹¹ In Isa. 52:13 the Palestinian Syriac version renders "my servant" by *ṭalyī*. Cf. J. Jeremias *Theological Dictionary of the New Testament*, E. T., v (Grand Rapids, 1968), p. 702, n. 356 (*s.v.* παῖς θεοῦ).

53:7 f., welcomes the help of Philip, who "beginning with this scripture
... told him the good news of Jesus".[1] Moreover, Luke is the only one
of the four evangelists who credits Jesus with an explicit quotation from
the fourth Servant Song, although the context in which he does so has
perplexed many commentators. Before leaving the upper room with His
disciples for the Mount of Olives, Jesus reminds them that, when He
formerly sent them out to preach "with no purse or bag or sandals", they
nevertheless lacked nothing. But now, said He,

> let him who has a purse take it, and likewise a bag. And let him who has no
> sword sell his mantle and buy one. For I tell you that this scripture must be
> fulfilled in me, "And he was reckoned with transgressors"; for what is written
> about me has its fulfilment.[2]

In other words, they would henceforth need more substantial equipment
than they had required hitherto. Their Master was about to be condemned
as a law-breaker and they would find themselves outlaws: they could no
longer count on the charity of sympathetic fellow-Israelites. If they were
to be classed as bandits by the authorities, they might as well act the part
properly; hence His reference to a sword. But when He saw that they had
failed to catch His meaning and took His words over-literally, He said
"Enough of this!" and dropped the subject.

The same words, "And he was reckoned with transgressors", are present
in later manuscripts and versions of Mark's passion narrative (but not on
the lips of Jesus) as fulfilled when two bandits were crucified with Him.
This set the pattern for the traditional Christian use of this particular
testimonium, but it cannot be regarded as part of the authentic text of
Mark.[3]

In all the Lukan references to the fourth Servant Song, no weight is laid
on the sin-bearing rôle of the Servant. The repeated emphasis on the necessity
of the Messiah's suffering is closely associated with the proclamation
of forgiveness of sins in his name, but that this forgiveness is the effect of
the Servant-Messiah's bearing the sins of men, while it may arguably be
implied, does not come to expression.

What is not expressed in Luke's writing, however, is clearly stated elsewhere
in the New Testament – not that we should make every mention of
Christ as sin-bearer dependent on Isaiah 53. Paul, especially in places where
he has been judged on other grounds to reproduce established confessional
statements or summaries of the apostolic preaching, provides several examples:
"our Lord Jesus Christ ... gave himself for our sins";[4] "for our

---

[1] Acts 8:26 ff.
[2] Luke 22:35-8; see T. W. Manson, *Ethics and the Gospel* (London, 1960), p. 90.
[3] Mark 15:28 (AV). Earlier in the Markan passion narrative (14:65) we have a fairly certain reminiscence of the third Servant Song (Isa. 50:6, LXX, with its reference to blows and spitting).
[4] Gal. 1:3 f.

Qumran (2nd century B.C.), "I have anointed (*māshaḥtī*) his face more than any man's";[1] but from later centuries we have allusions to Messiah in terms of the suffering Servant. For example, in a passage in the tractate *Sanhedrin* in the Babylonian Talmud the various names suggested for the Messiah are discussed, and this opinion is mentioned among others:

> The Messiah... what is his name?... Our rabbis say "the Leper (Aram. *ḥiwerā*) of the house of Rabbi (house of learning) is his name", as it is said: "Surely he has borne our sicknesses and carried our pains, yet we esteemed him a leper (Heb. *nāgūaʿ*, 'stricken'), smitten by God, and afflicted".[2]

More striking still is a passage in a hymn by the poet Eleazar ben Qalir (variously dated from the late seventh to the tenth century A.D.) which is included in the additional prayers for the Day of Atonement:

> Our righteous Messiah has departed from us;
> we are horror-stricken, and there is none to justify us.
> Our iniquities and the yoke of our transgressions
> he carries, and is wounded for our transgressions.
> He bears on his shoulder our sins
> to find pardon for our iniquities
> may we be healed by his stripes!

Such allusions probably reflect a tradition antedating the controversy between Jews and Christians on Old Testament interpretation.

4. *The Servant in the New Testament*

Our chief concern, however, is with the New Testament application of the Servant Songs. The fourth Song in particular lay ready to hand for the earliest preachers of the gospel to use as a *testimonium* of the passion of Jesus, showing that, although He fell victim to the malice of His enemies, He was nevertheless "delivered up according to the definite plan and foreknowledge of God".[3] The writings of Luke, which have already furnished us with examples of the Christian use of the second Song, do the same service in respect of the fourth. Peter, in the earliest days of the apostolic preaching, addressing the crowd that had gathered in the temple court because of the healing of the lame man who sat begging at the Beautiful Gate, announces that "the God of Abraham and of Isaac and of Jacob, the God of our fathers, glorified his servant Jesus"[4] – and thus serves notice that Jesus is the Servant who has been "exalted and lifted up" by God as a sequel to humiliation, suffering and death. Later in Luke's narrative the Ethiopian chancellor, beguiling his journey back from Jerusalem with the reading of "the prophet Isaiah" and puzzled by the language of chapter

---

[1] Cf. W. H. Brownlee, "The Servant of the Lord in the Qumran Scrolls", *BASOR* 132 (December 1953), pp. 8 ff.; *BASOR* 135 (October 1954), pp. 33 ff.
[2] TB *Sanhedrin* 98b.   [3] Acts 2:23.   [4] Acts 3:13.

The speaker seems to think of himself figuratively as a leper; the word translated "stricken" is the same as that used in Isaiah 53:4, "yet we esteemed him stricken" (Hebrew *nāgūaʻ*), where a reference (whether figurative or not) to leprosy has frequently been diagnosed since rabbinical times at least.[1]

These quotations from the Qumran *Hymns* confirm the impression made by passages in companion documents that the members of the community were conscious of a vocation to fulfil the commission of the Servant of Yahweh.

A different interpretation appears in the Septuagint, where the opening words of the first Servant Song take the form, "Jacob my servant, I will help him; Israel my chosen one, my soul has accepted him". On the other hand the Aramaic Targum on the Prophets – which, while committed to writing perhaps as late as the fifth century A.D., embodies much earlier tradition – glosses the first mention of the Servant quite differently: "Behold my servant Messiah,[2] I will bring him near". Similarly the fourth Song begins in this Targum: "Behold my servant Messiah will prosper."[3] But the Targumist is very far from admitting a suffering Messiah; the sufferings described in the fourth Song are predicted by him either of the Jewish people enduring oppression at the hand of their Gentile overlords or of their oppressors receiving retribution at the hand of the Messiah. The Messiah champions his people against the Gentiles and if, like the Servant, he delivers up his soul to death, he does so by risking his life in battle on his people's behalf. This insertion of an interpretative word alongside "Servant" – whether of "Israel" in the Septuagint or of "Messiah" in the Targum – may be compared with the practice of Paul who, when the Scripture lessons were read in the synagogue at Corinth, interpreted them (according to the Western text) by "inserting the name of the Lord Jesus".[4]

The Targumist's careful avoidance of any suggestion of vicarious suffering on the part of Messiah may represent a reaction against the well-established Christian interpretation; it has been held that another effect of this reaction is the absence of the fourth Song from the prophetic lessons read in synagogue as supplements to the lessons from the Torah.[5] But traces of a tradition of a suffering Messiah are present in Judaism. We should perhaps not attach too much importance to the striking reading of Isaiah 52:14 in the complete Hebrew scroll of Isaiah from Cave 1 at

---

[1] See p. 89, 94.
[2] Not in all manuscripts of the Targum; the gloss in Isa 42:1 is absent from the editions of J. F. Stenning and A. Sperber.
[3] The Targum also glosses "my servant" in Isa. 43:10 (not in a Servant Song) with "Messiah". It interprets Isa. 49:1–6 of Israel and Isa. 50:4–7 of the prophet himself.
[4] Acts 18:4.
[5] Cf. H. Loewe in C. G. Montefiore and H. Loewe, *A Rabbinic Anthology* (London, 1938), p. 544.

The judgement committed to these elect ones is evidently executed in association with the Son of Man of the *Similitudes*, who is himself described as the Elect One and the Righteous One, although prior suffering is not expressly predicted of him as it is of them.[1]

If we look for recognizable quotations from the Servant Songs (as distinct from echoes of their thought and language) in the Qumran texts, we shall find them chiefly in the *Hymns of Thanksgiving*, several passages in which are influenced in particular by the third Song. (There is, of course, no indication that the men of Qumran linked this Song as closely with the others as we do.) In these passages the language is cast in the first person singular: the "I" who speaks in them has been variously interpreted as the unknown composer of this or that hymn; the Teacher of Righteousness, viewed as the author of some if not all of the hymns; the spokesman of the community or the corporate personality of the community. We hear him say, for example:

> My tongue is as that of those who are taught by thee.[2]

Or again, with reference to an occasion on which the speaker could not discharge his ministry:

> I could not raise my voice
> [With the tong]ue of those who are taught [by thee],
> To revive the spirit of the stumbling,
> Or to sustain with a word him that is weary.[3]

The following passage is reminiscent of the second Song:

> For thou knowest me from (? better than) my father,
> And from the womb [thou hast set me apart];
> [Yea, from the body of] my mother thou hast dealt bountifully with me,
> And from the breast of her who conceived me thy tender mercies have been upon me.
> In the bosom of my nurse [thou hast sustained me],
> And from my youth thou hast enlightened me in the understanding of thy judgements;
> With thy truth thou hast firmly supported me,
> And in thy holy spirit thou hast made me rejoice.[4]

And this owes something to the fourth Song:

> [My] dwelling-place is with diseases,
> And my resting-place among those that are stricken;
> And I am as a man forsaken.[5]

---

[1] The Son of Man is finally identified in the *Similitudes* with Enoch himself (I Enoch 71:14); in Wisdom 4:10–15 (cf. 2:12–20) Enoch serves in part as the model for the righteous "servant of the Lord" who is exposed to unmerited persecution.
[2] 1 QH 7.10.
[3] 1 QH 8.35 f.
[4] 1 QH 9.29–32.
[5] 1 QH 8.26 f.

farther and recall that the *maśkīlīm* of Daniel's last vision are identical with the "saints of the Most High" of an earlier vision, who suffer severely for a limited period under the "little horn" (Antiochus Epiphanes) and who, in the angelic interpretation of Daniel's vision of judgement, are the counterpart to the "one like a son of man" in the vision itself?[1]

These questions would probably have remained unanswered – indeed they might not have been asked at all – but for the evidence that the Qumran community, spiritual heirs of Daniel's *maśkīlīm*, apparently regarded themselves as called upon corporately to fulfil what was written concerning the Servant of the Lord. The privations which the members of the community accepted in their study and practice of the holy law, the persecutions which they endured at the hands of the Wicked Priest and other ungodly oppressors, were regarded by them as accumulating a treasury of merit which would be set to the credit of their misguided fellow-countrymen and effect atonement for their polluted land. Those who endured to the end would be saved, like Daniel's *maśkīlīm*, and constitute the latter-day congregation of Israel – "the men of God's counsel who kept his covenant in the midst of wickedness, so as to make atonement for the land".[2] The designation *maśkīl* recurs in Qumran literature in the sense of "teacher", and this should probably serve as sufficient reason for treating the term as causative when it appears in Daniel, rather than translating it "wise" as does RSV.

If the men of Qumran endeavoured to fulfil the ministry of the Servant of Yahweh during the "era of wickedness", it is evident that they looked forward to fulfilling the rôle of the "one like a son of man" (although this designation is not expressly quoted) when the end-time came, executing judgement on the ungodly: "into the hand of his elect will God commit the judgement of all nations, and by the chastisement which they inflict those who have kept his commandments in the time of their distress will destroy all the wicked of his people."[3] Similarly in the *Similitudes of Enoch* the body of people variously denominated "the elect", "the holy" and "the righteous" are called not only to suffering but also in due course to the execution of judgement:

> In those days the kings of the earth shall become downcast in countenance,
> Even the strong who possess the land because of the works of their hands;
> For on the day of their anguish and affliction they shall not save themselves,
> And I will give them over into the hands of my elect:
> As straw in the fire they shall burn in the presence of the holy:
> As lead in the water they shall sink in the presence of the righteous,
> And no trace of them shall be found for evermore.[4]

---

[1] Dan. 7:21 ff.
[2] 1 Q Sa 1.3. See F. F. Bruce, *Biblical Exegesis in the Qumran Texts* (London, 1960), pp. 57 ff.
[3] 1 Q p Hab 5.4–6.
[4] 1 Enoch 48:8 f. See p. 27 above.

of Yahweh?").[1] But no Israelite king or ruler known to Old Testament history or literature meets the case; some of those suggested do not even begin to meet it. While the Servant is sometimes spoken of in the past tense, the principal part of his ministry lies in the future. His ministry to Israel and the nations corresponds with that of the coming king whose advent, according to Isaiah 55:3-5, means the fulfilment of the covenant-mercies promised to David. It may help to confirm this identification if we compare the language in which the Servant is introduced in the first Servant Song with that in which the "shoot from the stump of Jesse", the promised Davidic Messiah, is described in Isaiah 11:1-10. On the Davidic Messiah and the Servant alike the Spirit of Yahweh rests; both administer justice equitably, among the nations as well as in Israel.

The earliest interpretation of the Servant is perhaps that passage in Isaiah 61 where the speaker tells how Yahweh has anointed him to bring good tidings to the afflicted and proclaim the year of Yahweh's favour. A later interpretation may be recognized in the pierced one of Zechariah 12:10 at whom we shall look more particularly in a further study.[2] We have already suggested that another identification is to be recognized in the book of Daniel.[3]

In the last vision of Daniel mention is made of men called the *maśkīlīm*, those who impart wisdom to the people, teaching them how to keep the law of their God aright. On them falls the full weight of the persecution under Antiochus Epiphanes: they "fall by sword and flame, by captivity and plunder, for some days".[4] So severe is the persecution that some of their number fall away, but their defection means the purification of those who remain, "to refine and to cleanse them and to make them white, until the time of the end".[5] When that time comes, and the new resurrection age dawns, the *maśkīlīm* "shall shine like the brightness of the firmament; and those who turn the many to righteousness, like the stars for ever and ever".[6] The form *maśkīlīm* is the plural of the Hiph'il (causative) participle of the same verb as appears in the Hiph'il imperfect at the beginning of the fourth Servant Song, where it is announced that the Servant "shall prosper" (RSV) or "deal wisely" (Heb. *yaśkīl*).[7] This might be regarded as nothing but a coincidence, were it not that the phrase which stands in synonymous parallelism with *maśkīlīm* in Daniel 12:3, "those who turn the many to righteousness", reminds us of the statement in Isaiah 53:11 that the Servant will "make the many to be accounted righteous". Are we intended to recognize in Daniel's *maśkīlīm* a corporate fulfilment of the Isaianic Servant? And would it be too hazardous to go

---

[1] To document these various suggested identifications would involve a potted history of the exegesis of the Servant Songs: see C. R. North, *The Suffering Servant in Deutero-Isaiah*² (Oxford, 1956); V. de Leeuw, *De Ebed Jahweh-Profetieen* (Louvain/Paris, 1956); H. H. Rowley, *The Servant of the Lord and Other Essays on the Old Testament*² (Oxford, 1965), pp. 1-93.

[2] See pp. 110f.   [3] See pp. 29 f.   [4] Dan. 11:33.
[5] Dan. 11:35.   [6] Dan. 12:3.   [7] Isa. 52:13.

contrast with the "bad figs", the people who remained behind under Zedekiah.¹ Nor is it likely that the prophet speaks of himself, as the Ethiopian chancellor thought possible,² or of some other prophet, such as Jeremiah. True, Jeremiah compares himself to "a gentle lamb led to the slaughter" (a simile used of the Servant in the fourth Song) but far from enduring his persecution uncomplainingly he prays for Yahweh's vengeance on his persecutors.³ In some respects Jeremiah's contemporary Ezekiel comes closer to the character of the Servant, when by divine command he "bears the punishment" of the houses of Israel and Judah.⁴ But none of these prophets was a figure of international significance such as the Servant is.

There is one man who could be closely identified with his nation and yet be distinct from it, who by virtue of his special relation to it could bear its sin, even, if necessary, sacrificing his life for it, who could at the same time be taken note of by nations and their rulers; that is the king.⁵ In ancient societies with a sacral kingship this was especially true; the king was not only his people's representative before God and men but was a representative of God to his people – in Israel, Yahweh's anointed one. The king in earlier days discharged priestly as well as royal functions: King David, for example, acted as priest and prophet. The Servant, as has been said above, is a prophet, declaring the will of God; he is a priest, "sprinkling many nations"⁶ with water of purification; much that is otherwise difficult to understand in his portrayal becomes explicable if he is recognized also as Israel's king.

But which king? Several rulers of earlier days have been suggested: Moses, that consummate intercessor; Uzziah, who contracted leprosy⁷ in the holy house when he was about to offer incense on the altar; Jehoiachin who surrendered at discretion to Nebuchadrezzar and thus saved his city then such sufferings as befell it eleven years later; Zerubbabel his grandson, who disappears from history after his few years as governor of Judah under the Persians; or Zerubbabel's son Meshullam, of whom we know nothing except that his name is identical with the word rendered "dedicated one" in Isaiah 42:19 ("Who is blind as my dedicated one, or blind as the servant

---

¹ Jer. 24:1 ff.   ² Acts 8:34.   ³ Jer. 11:19 f.; cf. 18:19 ff.

⁴ Ezek. 4:4 ff.; "no prophet, not even Jeremiah, so completely identified himself with the sins and sufferings of Israel as Ezekiel did" (S. H. Hooke, *The Kingdom of God in the Experience of Jesus*, London, 1949, p. 61).

⁵ Cf. I. Engnell, "The Ebed Yahweh Songs and the Suffering Messiah in Deutero-Isaiah", *BJRL* 31 (1948), pp. 1 ff. "We are not committing ourselves to a mythological interpretation of the Servant Songs in recognizing that the Tammuz imagery and phraseology which Engnell finds in the Songs is being gathered up and transformed into spiritual terms in the great substitute figure of the Ebed-Jahveh" (S. H. Hooke, *The Siege Perilous*, London, 1956, p. 221).

⁶ It is best to retain this rendering for *yazzeh* in Isa. 52:15, even if "the meaning of the Hebrew word is uncertain" (so RSV, which renders it "startle"). See W. H. Brownlee, "The Servant of the Lord in the Qumran Scrolls", *BASOR* 132 (December 1953), pp. 8 ff., esp. p. 10; E. J. Young, *Studies in Isaiah* (Grand Rapids, 1954), pp. 199 ff.

⁷ For the interpretation of *nāgūaʿ* ("stricken") in Isa. 53:4 of leprosy see pp. 93 f. below.

> Behold, my servant shall prosper,
>> he shall be exalted and lifted up,
>> and shall he very high.
> As many were astonished at him –
>> his appearance was so marred, beyond human semblance,
>> and his form beyond that of the sons of men –
> so shall he sprinkle many nations;
>> kings shall shut their mouths because of him;
> for that which has not been told them they shall see,
>> and that which they have not heard they shall understand.[1]

The isolation of the four Servant Songs from their context is the work of modern criticism; we need not expect ancient readers to have distinguished them as as we have learned to do. It is plain, for example, that in New Testament times the whole of Isaiah 40–66 was recognized as a connected *testimonium*, or at least a rich source of *testimonia*, for the gospel story, from the voice of Isaiah 40:3 which calls for the preparation of Yahweh's way in the wilderness (quoted by the Evangelists in their account of John the Baptist)[2] to the announcement of new heavens and a new earth in Isaiah 65:17 and 66:22.[3] But it would be natural for readers of any age to conclude that it was one and the same person who was twice introduced by Yahweh with the words "Behold my servant", at the beginning of the first and fourth Servant Songs, as we call them.[4]

3. The Servant's Identity

Who is this Servant? He is manifestly not Cyrus: Cyrus fulfilled Yahweh's purpose, indeed, but not because he recognized and accepted it as such and not by the way of humiliation and suffering. The Servant is closely associated with Israel and on one occasion is actually addressed as Israel, yet his mission is directed in part towards Israel and it is for Israel's transgressions that he endures his suffering. The afflictions of Israel, according to the prophet, were due to Israel's transgression – Jerusalem "has received from Yahweh's hand double for all her sins"[5] – but the afflictions of the Servant, according to the same prophet, were due to the transgression of others. Israel receives Yahweh's salvation, but the Servant is the agent by whom this salvation is conveyed.

The Servant is a figure of whom kings and nations take distinct cognizance; this appears to rule out those views which identify him with the ideal Israel or with a group within Israel – the exiles of the first deportation, for example, distinguished as "good figs" in one of Jeremiah's oracles by

---
[1] Isa. 52:13–15.   [2] Mark 1:3 and parallels; John 1:23.
[3] Cf. II Peter 3:13; Rev. 21:1.
[4] Isa. 42:1; 52:13. The rabbinical interpretative principle *gᵉzērāh shāwāh* ("equal category") wo uld have suggested a unitive exegesis of the two passages so introduced.
[5] Isa. 40:2.

> which thou hast prepared in the presence of all peoples,
> a light for revelation to the Gentiles,
> and for glory to thy people Israel[1] –

and once in the synagogue at Pisidian Antioch, where Paul and Barnabas turn to the Gentiles because the Jewish community will have nothing to do with the gospel, and justify their action thus:

> For so the Lord has commanded us, saying,
> "I have set you to be a light for the Gentiles,
> that you may bring salvation to the
> uttermost parts of the earth".[2]

Luke's personal interest in the Gentile mission is sufficient explanation of the prominence he gives to this theme.

The Servant's election, according to his own testimony in the third Song, involves daily obedience, as is but natural, but also outrageous abuse:

> The Lord Yahweh has opened my ear,
> and I was not rebellious,
> I turned not backward.
> I gave my back to the smiters,
> and my cheeks to those who pulled out the beard;
> I hid not my face
> from shame and spitting.[3]

But he endures this suffering steadfastly because of his faith in God: God will vindicate him against his adversaries, and he knows that he will not be put to shame.

For this suffering, as the fourth Song shows clearly, is the indispensable means by which the Servant completes the mission entrusted to him by his God. Those who witness his suffering imagine at first that he has incurred the signal displeasure of God, so terrible are his afflictions, so unsightly do they render him. Later they recognize that his suffering was vicarious, that the afflictions he endured represented the judgement which their sins had accumulated but which the Servant absorbed in his own person. By the very endurance of sickness, oppression and unjust death he fulfils his divinely appointed commission. From the darkness of death he comes forth to the light of new life, and his bearing the iniquity of others now ensures God's acceptance of "the many" as righteous.[4] By submission to humiliation and death "for the transgression of my people to whom the stroke was due",[5] by accepting the rôle of a sin-offering[6] when he yielded up his life, he has won the triumph both for himself and for those whose cause he undertook. Therefore this fourth Song is introduced by Yahweh in language which anticipates the final triumph:

[1] Luke 2:30–32 (see p. 78 above). Cf. Acts 26:23.
[2] Acts 13:47.   [3] Isa. 50:5 f.   [4] Isa. 53:11.   [5] Isa. 53:8.
[6] Isa. 53:10 (Heb. *'āshām*, "reparation-offering"); see p. 96, n. 2).

unjust judgement, contempt, suffering and death. Such a fate is the reward meted out to him by others for his obedience to God, but it is more than that: it is the crowning act of his obedience; it is the very means by which he fulfils the purpose of God in a more abiding fashion than Cyrus could ever achieve, and in consequence brings blessing and liberation to multitudes.

It is such a programme as this that, according to the Evangelists, Jesus set Himself to fulfil. The actual words of the first Servant Song are quoted with reference to His healing activity in the Gospel of Matthew,[1] but without quoting them explicitly the other Evangelists indicate that their spirit informed the course of His ministry. One of the wilderness temptations, in which universal dominion is offered to Him, as it had been to many a conqueror before, in return for the worship of the archon of this world-order, results in His repudiation of the way of Cyrus and Alexander and Caesar – and for that matter the way of King David himself – in favour of the way of the Servant, which represented both His Father's will for Him and His own fixed purpose.[2]

2. *The Servant's Mission*

If the first Servant Song presents the Servant as the Elect One of God, endowed with His Spirit to make known His truth to the world, in the second Song the Servant himself tells how he was chosen from birth for this purpose, and commissioned by God in these words:

> It is too light a thing that you should be my servant
> to raise up the tribes of Jacob
> and to restore the preserved of Israel;
> I will give you as a light to the nations,
> that my salvation may reach to the end of the earth.[3]

Although in the context of the Songs the nation of Israel as such is called Yahweh's servant, Israel as a whole is a blind and deaf servant.[4] The Servant of the Songs is closely associated with Israel; indeed, in this second Song he is actually addressed by Yahweh as Israel:

> You are my servant,
> Israel, in whom I will be glorified.[5]

But while the Servant is in some sense the representative or embodiment of Israel, he is distinguished from the nation as a whole, to which indeed his mission is first directed, as well as (thereafter) to the Gentile world.

Twice in Luke's history the description of the Servant as a light to the Gentiles is quoted: once in the nativity narrative where Simeon in the temple hails the infant Jesus as the salvation of God,

---

[1] Matt. 8:17.   [2] Matt. 4:8–10 // Luke 4:5–8.
[3] Isa. 49:6.   [4] Isa. 42:19.   [5] Isa. 49:3.

> They shall build up the ancient ruins,
> > they shall raise up the former devastations;
> they shall repair the ruined cities,
> > the devastations of many generations.[1]

On the speaker here, as on the Servant in the first Song, Yahweh has put His Spirit, but here the endowment with the Spirit is described as Yahweh's "anointing" him. The speaker is thus in some sense a Messiah (the verb he uses is *māshaḥ*). It may be in reminiscence of this passage that Peter, in Acts 10:38, tells Cornelius and his household "how God anointed Jesus of Nazareth with the Holy Spirit and with power"; it is more than a reminiscence that we find in the first part of Luke's history when Jesus, that sabbath day in Nazareth, chooses the second lesson from the scroll of the prophet Isaiah, reading the first few clauses of Isaiah 61, but stopping short at "the year of Yahweh's favour" and announcing to the astonished congregation: "Today this scripture has been fulfilled in your hearing".[2] In both these Lukan passages the anointing is equated with the descent of the Spirit on Jesus at His baptism. Elsewhere in the Gospels the baptism of Jesus is brought into close association with the first Servant Song, not only by the descent of the Spirit, which appears in all the strands of Gospel tradition, but by the words addressed to Jesus by the heavenly voice as He comes up out of Jordan: "Thou art my Son, my beloved; with thee I am well pleased".[3] If "Thou art my Son", from the oracle in Psalm 2:7, acclaims Him as Yahweh's Anointed, the words that follow, drawn from Yahweh's opening presentation of His Servant, indicate the character of the messianic mission. This mission is not to follow the traditional lines of military Messiahship: it is to be that appointed for the Servant:

> He will not cry or lift up his voice,
> > or make it heard in the street;
> a bruised reed he will not break,
> > and a dimly burning wick he will not quench;
> > he will faithfully bring forth justice.
> He will not fail or be discouraged
> > till he has established justice in the earth;
> > and the coastlands wait for his law.[4]

Cyrus has served Yahweh unconsciously; here is one who will serve Him willingly and intelligently. Cyrus has served the divine purpose by the temporary and limited methods of military conquest and imperial power; here is one who will serve it in a far different way – not by making a noise in the world but in obscurity and by patient obedience; not by the imposition of his will on others but by uncomplaining endurance of

---
[1] Isa. 61:1-4.   [2] Luke 4:16-21.
[3] Mark 1:10 f. It is against this background that we must understand the repeated "If you are the Son of God" of the temptation narrative (Matt. 4:3, 6 // Luke 4:3, 9).
[4] Isa. 42:2-4.

position of world dominion in which he may perform Yahweh's pleasure and restore the Jewish exiles to their homeland. The purpose and effect of this will be that all nations shall know that Yahweh is God alone. The good tidings thus proclaimed to Zion will find an echo throughout the whole world; they involve, in fact, good tidings for all mankind.[1]

But how can the rise of a heathen conqueror, how indeed can the return of a few thousand displaced Jews, have such world-wide religious implications? Because by these movements, whatever their intrinsic importance may be, the stage is set for something more important still – for the introduction of a figure who puts Cyrus in the shade, the Servant of Yahweh whose direct mission it is to spread the knowledge of the true God to the ends of the earth.

This Servant is introduced by Yahweh in Isaiah 42:1:

> Behold my servant, whom I uphold
>   my chosen, in whom my soul delights;
> I have put my Spirit upon him,
>   he will bring justice to the nations.

Four passages in the Book of Consolation have been distinguished as "Servant Songs" in which this figure appears, whether introduced by Yahweh, as here, or speaking in his own person, or described by others. These passages are (a) Isaiah 42:1–4 (with verses 5–9 as a connecting link with what follows), (b) 49:1–6 (with verses 7–13 as a connecting link), (c) 50:4–9 (possibly with verses 10, 11 as a connecting link), (d) 52:13–53:12. In addition to these, there is an oracle in the chapters which follow the Book of Consolation which, while it is not usually reckoned among the Servant Songs proper, breathes the same sentiments and almost certainly was intended by its author to express the mind and mission of the Servant of the Songs:

> The Spirit of the Lord Yahweh is upon me,
>   because Yahweh has anointed me
> bo bring good tidings to the afflicted;
>   he has sent me to bind up the brokenhearted,
> to proclaim liberty to the captives,
>   and the opening of the prison to those who are bound;
> to proclaim the year of Yahweh's favour,
>   and the day of vengeance of our God;
> to comfort all who mourn;
> to grant to those who mourn in Zion –
>   to give them a garland instead of ashes,
> the oil of gladness instead of mourning,
>   the mantle of praise instead of a faint spirit;
> that they may be called oaks of righteousness,
>   the planting of Yahweh, that he may be glorified.

---

[1] Isa. 41:2 f., 25; 44:28–45:7.

CHAPTER VII

THE SERVANT MESSIAH

"About whom, pray, does the prophet say this, about himself or about some one else?"

WHEN, IN ISAIAH 55:3, THE RETURNING JUDAEAN EXILES ARE PROMised the restoration of "the holy and sure blessings of David", this promise is followed at once by the words:

> Behold, I made him a witness to the peoples,
> a leader and commander to the peoples.[1]

This must be a reference to David, who did in fact exercise overlordship over many of his Gentile neighbours; but the submission of the Gentiles in the age of restoration will be voluntary, not compelled by military force or diplomatic pressure:

> Behold, you shall call nations that you know not,
> and nations that knew you not shall run to you,
> because of Yahweh your God, even the Holy One of Israel,
> for he has glorified you.[2]

These promises come towards the end of the Book of Consolation (Isaiah 40–55) which includes, as its most distinctive feature, the four Servant Songs. They do not occur in a Servant Song, but they are so completely in keeping with the theme of the Songs that they cannot well be interpreted in isolation from them. Indeed, the new "leader and commander to the peoples" in whom, as these promises imply, the "holy and sure blessings of David" are to be fulfilled may with high probability be identified with the Servant of the Songs.

1. *The Servant Introduced*

To bring about the repatriation of His exiled people to their Judaean homeland, promised at the beginning of the Book of Consolation, Yahweh tells how He has raised up Cyrus, founder of the Persian Empire. As Cyrus marches from victory to victory, he does not realize that his conquering progress is directed by a power that he does not know, the power of the one true God, by contrast with whom all the gods of the nations are nonentities. Yet, in spite of Cyrus's ignorance, Yahweh, Israel's God, has anointed him and held his right hand, in order to bring him to a

---

[1] Isa. 55:4.   [2] Isa. 55:5.

highly exalted by God.[1] Great David's greater Son reigns, more gloriously than great David himself ever did, as Prophet and Priest and King; but He bears this triple dignity as the Servant of Yahweh who crowned His service by "pouring out his soul to death".[2]

[1] Acts 2:32 ff.; 3:13 ff.; 4:10 ff.; 5:30 f.; 10:39 ff.; 13:27 ff.; Eph. 1:20 ff.; Phil. 2:8 ff.
[2] Isa. 53:12, reproduced in Phil. 2:7 f., where the one who took "the form of a servant" is said to have "emptied himself ... unto death".

see the Son of man sitting at the right hand of Power, and coming with the clouds of heaven."[1] No such unambiguous answer to the question had been given before. At Caesarea Philippi Jesus accepted the title when Peter used it of Him, but warned Peter and the other disciples not to tell any one that He was the Messiah.[2] This reticence is only to be expected in the Markan record with its "messianic secret"; but even in the Fourth Gospel, where the earliest phases of the ministry are seen in the light of the ultimate revelation, Jesus is so far from committing Himself that, only four months before His trial, the authorities in Jerusalem have still to say to Him: "How long will you keep us in suspense? If you are the Christ, tell us plainly"[3] – and no straight "Yes" or "No" is given on this occasion. The popular associations of the titles "Messiah" and "Son of David" would cause misunderstanding and undesirable trouble if they were publicly claimed. Only when the ministry reached its climax in a victory of a very different kind from that which the Messiah of popular expectation was to win was it possible for such titles, reinterpreted in the light of that event, to be used without connotations that would detract from Jesus' true dignity.

The claim to be Messiah would not be blasphemy in itself, if it constituted a claim to be no more than the son of David. But in replying to the high priest's question Jesus went on to use language drawn from the judgement scene of Daniel 7, where "one like a son of man" comes with the clouds of heaven to receive universal and everlasting dominion from the Ancient of Days.[4] His judges took this to mean that He claimed much more than Davidic sonship – that He claimed, in effect, to be the peer of the Most High. This was blasphemy indeed, in their eyes.[5]

Jesus would not be the kind of Messiah that many of His people wanted Him to be, and they would not have the only kind of Messiah that He was prepared to be. His judges could not believe that He was the Lord's Anointed, and they pronounced Him deserving of the death penalty. Were they right or wrong? The apostolic preaching gave an emphatic answer to the question. God had indeed sent Him, and God raised Him up from the dead. But by so doing God did not simply reverse the verdict of an earthly court. He brought His ancient purpose and promise to fulfilment. Jesus of Nazareth, crucified by men, said the apostles, has been

---

[1] Mark 14:62 (see pp. 28 ff.); the parallel passages in Matt. 26:64 ("You have said so") and Luke 22:70 ("You say that I am") put the responsibility for the framing of the question in messianic terms on the high priest and his colleagues; the Markan version of Jesus' reply does something similar by showing how He immediately re-worded their language in terms of His own, which made it clear in what sense He accepted the messianic rôle for Himself.

[2] Mark 8:29 f. and parallels.   [3] John 10:24.

[4] Daniel 7:13 f.; see p. 26 above.

[5] Mark 14:64. One strand of interpretation (whether known in Judaea or not we cannot say) is preserved in the oldest extant Greek version of Daniel 7:13, where the "one like a son of man" comes not "to" but "as the Ancient of Days" (cf. Rev. 1:13 ff.,where some of the features of "one like a son of man" are drawn from the portrayal of the Ancient of Days of Daniel 7:9 f.). See p. 107, n. 3.

the sacrifice of his own life – that the Lion of the tribe of Judah has conquered: once more, the Messiah takes on the lineaments of the Suffering Servant.[1]

5. Jesus and the Son of David

In view of the pervasive emphasis on Jesus' Davidic descent in so many strata of the New Testament, we cannot fail to be impressed by the almost complete absence of this emphasis from His own teaching. This suggests, among other things, that the Gospel tradition of His teaching did not import into it elements from the mind of the early church so indiscriminately as is frequently supposed. He did not repudiate the title "son of David" when it was given to Him by others,[2] and refused to rebuke the pilgrim crowds who used language of this kind when He rode into Jerusalem on an ass.[3] His self-portrayal as the true shepherd of the flock in John 10 has as part of its Old Testament background the oracle of Ezekiel where Yahweh appoints "my servant David" to take charge of His sheep,[4] but the Davidic association is not mentioned in John 10, and there is another important part of the Old Testament background of Jesus' depiction as a shepherd which will engage our attention later.[5]

It is plain that, whatever Old Testament authority Jesus invoked in vindication of His ministry, those passages which speak of the restoration of David's kingdom were not used for this purpose. On the one occasion when He is recorded as taking the initiative in raising the subject of the son of David, it was to emphasize that there was a more important aspect of the Messiah's character than could be expressed by this designation.

> How can the scribes say that the Christ is the son of David? David himself, inspired by the Holy Spirit, declared,
> > "The Lord said to my Lord,
> > Sit at my right hand,
> > till I put thy enemies under thy feet."
> David himself calls him Lord; so how is he his son?[6]

Implicit in these words is a suggestion of the divine dignity of the Messiah, as there is also in the words of Jesus' reply to the high priest's question at His trial: "Are you the Christ, the Son of the Blessed?"[7] Why not "Are you the Christ, the son of David?" Perhaps because an affirmative reply to this would not have had the theological implication that such a reply to the actual question would have. "I am", was the reply, "and you will

---

[1] Rev. 5:6 ff. (cf. 12:11).   [2] Cf. Mark 10:47 f.; Matt. 15:22.
[3] Cf. Mark 11:10 // Matt. 21:9.
[4] John 10:11 ff.; cf. Ezek. 34:23 f. (see pp. 74, n. 2; 101 with n. 3).
[5] Zech. 11:14 ff.; 14:7; see pp. 101 ff.
[6] Mark 12:35-37a, quoting Psalm 110:1.   [7] Mark 14:61b.

died and was buried, and his tomb is with us to this day. Being therefore a prophet, and knowing that God had sworn with an oath to him that he would set one of his descendants upon his throne, he foresaw and spoke of the resurrection of the Christ, that he was not abandoned to Hades, nor did his flesh see corruption. This Jesus God raised up, and of that we all are witnesses.[1]

James the Just at the Council of Jerusalem sees the restoration of David's fallen booth, foretold in Amos 9:11, fulfilled in the resurrection and exaltation of Jesus and in the reconstitution of His followers as a new community embracing believing Gentiles as well as believing Jews.[2] Through the Gentile mission non-Jews in many lands were gladly submitting to the sovereignty of the Son of David, and not only "the remnant of Edom" and the other nations which had paid tribute to David but (by grace of another vocalization of the Hebrew) "the rest of men" were now being called by the name of the God of Israel.[3] And the general sense of the New Testament interpretation of these Davidic oracles suggests that, just as the promise to build a house for David was fully realized not in Solomon but in Christ, so the prediction that David's son would build a house for God was consummated not in Solomon's temple but in the new temple of Christ's body in which His people "are built . . . for a dwelling place of God in the Spirit."[4]

Again, in the Epistle to the Hebrews, Jesus is viewed as the One to whom Yahweh in Psalm 110 says not only "Sit at my right hand" (so that the throne of David is now absorbed in the heavenly throne of glory and grace) but also "You are a priest for ever after the order of Melchizedek".[5] David, by his conquest of Jerusalem, became heir to Melchizedek's royal priesthood, but it is in the ascension and heavenly session of Jesus Christ that the fulness of this heritage is realized.[6]

In the Apocalypse Jesus is, like David in Psalm 89, "the first-born" – but the first-born in resurrection – and "the ruler of kings on earth".[7] He holds "the key of David" – not as chief steward in the royal palace, like Eliakim, but as ruler of the house.[8] He is the conquering "Lion of the tribe of Judah" (in terms of Jacob's blessing of that tribe) and "the Root of David" (harking back to Isaiah's "root of Jesse"),[9] and again, "the root and the offspring of David, the bright morning star" – which may echo Balaam's words about the "star . . . out of Jacob" which is to overthrow all the enemies of Israel.[10] But when we inquire into the means by which the victory is won in the Apocalypse, they are totally different from those which King David employed: it is in the rôle of the slaughtered Lamb – by

---

[1] Acts 2:29–32. [2] Acts 15:15–18.
[3] The Septuagint version of Amos 9:11, which is quoted in Acts, depends on a Hebrew text which read $yidr^e sh\bar{u}$ ("seek") instead of $y\bar{\imath}r^e sh\bar{u}$ ("possess") and $'\bar{a}\underline{d}\bar{a}m$ ("man") instead of $'\check{e}\underline{d}\bar{o}m$ ("Edom") and omitted before $sh^e'\bar{e}r\bar{\imath}\underline{t}$ ("remnant") the particle $'e\underline{t}$ which in the Massoretic text indicates that noun as being the definite object), so that it can be construed as subject.
[4] Eph. 2:22.   [5] Heb. 1:13; 5:6, etc.   [6] See p. 72, n. 1.   [7] Rev. 1:5.
[8] Rev. 3:7 (cf. Isa. 22:22; Heb. 3:2–6a).   [9] Rev. 5:5 (cf. Isa. 11:1, 10).
[10] Rev. 22:16b; cf. Num. 24:17 (see p. 76, n. 7).

and has raised up a horn of salvation for us
in the house of his servant David,
as he spoke by the mouth of his holy prophets from of old.[1]

The whole outlook and emphasis of these canticles are quite different from anything that Luke could have been expected to invent; they come from a circle where the hope of Israel was looked for in the form of a prince of the house of David, and where it was believed that this hope was on the point of fulfilment.

In the Lukan canticles, moreover, there are hints of an association between this prince of the house of David and another figure of Old Testament prophecy, the humble Servant of Yahweh[2] – an association which is perhaps implied in the original mention of the "holy and sure blessings of David" – but this will receive closer attention in the next chapter.

4. Fulfilment Announced

In the early preaching of the apostles, the statement that Jesus was a descendant of David recurs constantly. Paul, summing up the theme of the gospel in Romans 1:3, says that He "was descended from David according to the flesh". The genealogies of Matthew and Luke trace His ancestry by divergent routes, but the routes converge not only (as we have seen) in Zerubbabel, but also (and more pointedly) in David.[3] Nor does the Fourth Evangelist contradict this. He does indeed report a dispute in the temple court where some of the people assembled argue that Jesus cannot be the Messiah because He is a Galilaean, whereas the prophetic writings say that the Messiah "is descended from David, and comes from Bethlehem, the village where David was";[4] but to infer from this that John is denying the Davidic descent of Jesus, or His birth in Bethlehem, is to miss a subtle instance of Johannine irony.

The early Christian speeches outlined in the Acts of the Apostles bear the same testimony. The relevance of Paul's synagogue address at Pisidian Antioch has already been noted. Peter on the day of Pentecost quotes part of the sixteenth psalm and points out that it cannot refer to David in person:

Brethren, I may say to you confidently of the patriarch David, that he both

---

[1] Luke 1:68 ff.
[2] Simeon's *Nunc Dimittis* (Luke 2:29–32) echoes the language of the second Isaianic Servant Song (Isa. 49:6). See pp. 86 f.
[3] See p. 75 with n. 1. Matthew's tracing Jesus' lineage through the kings of the house of David from Solomon to Jeconiah (Jehoiachin) is calculated to assert Jesus' right to the throne of David. It is doubtful if the threefold "fourteen" of Matthew's reckoning (Matt. 1:17) should be related to the fact that the numerical value of the sum of the Hebrew letters in David's name is 14.
[4] John 7:41 f.

the throne of David",[1] but they have received due judgement at the hands of the Romans, who in their turn will be overthrown by the true Messiah. The programme of his reign is set forth in some detail on the basis of earlier oracles:

> See, Lord; raise up for them their king, the son of David,
> In a time which thou knowest, O God,
> that he may reign over Israel thy servant,
> And gird him with strength to dash in pieces the unjust rulers ...
> He will possess the nations, to serve him under his yoke,
> And he will glorify the Lord with the praise of all the earth.
> He will cleanse Jerusalem in holiness, as it was from the beginning,
> That the nations may come from the ends of the earth to see his glory,
> Bearing gifts for her sons that were utterly weakened,
> And to see the glory of the Lord wherewith God has glorified her.
> A righteous king, one taught by God, is he who rules over them,
> And there will be no unrighteousness among them all his days,
> For all will be holy, and their king is the Lord Messiah.[2]

The closing phrase of this quotation – "the Lord Messiah" or "the Anointed Lord" (Greek *christos kyrios*) – is identical with the title used in the angelic annunciation to the shepherds in Luke's nativity story: "to you is born this day in the city of David a Saviour, who is *Christ the Lord*".[3] To be sure, it has been suggested that in both places the original text had "the Lord's Anointed" (Greek *christos kyriou*, as in Luke 2:26); but this is no more than a conjecture.

The whole atmosphere of Luke's first two chapters, indeed, reminds us in some ways of the *Psalms of Solomon*; the pious people portrayed in these chapters (Zechariah and Elizabeth, Joseph and Mary, Simeon and Anna) apparently belonged to a group of "the quiet in the land" not unlike the group from which that psalter comes. And the canticles of these chapters in large measure celebrate the imminent fulfilment of the aspirations voiced in that psalter.[4] The note of fulfilment of the Davidic promises is sounded, for example, in Gabriel's annunciation to Mary about her Son:

> He will be great, and will be called the Son of the Most High:
> and the Lord God will give to him the throne of his father David:
> and he will reign over the house of Jacob for ever;
> and of his kingdom there will be no end.[5]

We hear the same note in Zechariah's *Benedictus*:

> Blessed be the Lord God of Israel:
> for he has visited and redeemed his people,

---

[1] Ps. Sol. 17:8. [2] Ps. Sol. 17:23 f., 32–36.
[3] Luke 2:11. In Lam. 4:20 LXX, "Yahweh's anointed" appears similarly as χριστὸς κύριος.
[4] See pp. 51 ff. above. [5] Luke 1:32 f.

Hasmonaeans,[1] the hope of Israel was conceived in various ways: for some the expectation of a deliverer from David's line was overshadowed by the expectation of one from the tribe of Levi, whether a Hasmonaean or a member of the family of Zadok which had been superseded by the Hasmonaeans. When, in one passage in the *Testaments of the Twelve Patriarchs*, we find the kingship bestowed on the tribe of Levi,[2] this is best explained by the fact that the Hasmonaean dynasty, which belonged to the tribe of Levi, combined the kingship with the high priesthood. Elsewhere in the *Testaments* the kingship and the priesthood are assigned to the tribes of Judah and Levi respectively, with the proviso that the kingship is as much inferior to the priesthood as the moon is to the sun.[3] This attitude harks back to Ezekiel's new commonwealth, in which the Davidic prince is subordinate to the priests.[4]

The same picture is found in some of the Qumran texts, where the royal Messiah of the new age ranks beneath the anointed priest (the "Messiah of Aaron"), the latter being head of state.[5] This is what might be expected in the outlook of a group in whose organization the priesthood (more particularly the Zadokite priesthood) played such a controlling part as in the Qumran community. But the Qumran community cherished the hope of the restoration of the Davidic monarchy: Jacob's blessing of Judah,[6] Balaam's vision of the star out of Jacob,[7] Nathan's promise to David,[8] Amos's prophecy of the re-erection of David's fallen booth,[9] Isaiah's description of the "shoot from the stump of Jesse",[10] are all interpreted of "the shoot ('Branch') of David, who is to stand up in the latter days"[11] – "the rightful Messiah, for to him and to his seed has been given the covenant of kingship over his people for everlasting generations."[12]

The end of the Hasmonaean period of independence, however, and the advent of Roman domination in 63 B.C., saw a revival of the ancient hope that deliverance would come from the house of David. From the early days of the Roman occupation of Judaea we have the collection of hymns known as the *Psalms of Solomon*, in which this revived hope finds clear expression. The Hasmonaean rulers are denounced for having "laid waste

---

[1] 142–63 B.C. [2] *Testament of Reuben* 6:7–12.
[3] *Testament of Judah* 21:1–5; *Testament of Naphtali* 5:1–3. When, however, we read in *Testament of Levi* 8:14 that "a king shall arise out of Judah and establish a new priesthood... for all the Gentiles", we have little difficulty in recognizing the hand of a Christian editor.
[4] Cf. Ezek. 45:7, 16 f., 22; 46:2, etc.; the "prince" is chief layman in a hierocracy.
[5] Cf. 1 Q Sa 2.11–22. [6] See p. 74, n. 1.
[7] Num. 24:17, quoted in 4 Q *Testimonia*, lines 9 ff.; 1 QM 11.4–6; CD 7.19–21.
[8] 4 Q *Florilegium*, col. 1, lines 1 ff.
[9] 4 Q *Florilegium* col. 1, lines 12 ff.; CD 7.16 f.
[10] 4 Q p Isa^a, fragment D: the Davidic Messiah of Isa. 11:1 will be the victorious leader in the "war against the Kittim".
[11] 4 Q p Isa^a, fragment D. In 4 Q *Florilegium*, col. 1, line 11, "the branch (ṣemaḥ) of David ... is to stand up with the Expounder of the Law [the eschatological priest?] ... in Zion in the last days".
[12] 4 Q *Patriarchal Blessings*, lines 3 f., following the words quoted in p. 74, n. 1.

righteous Branch" to be raised up for David, as foretold by Jeremiah, had not been forgotten; Zerubbabel's temporary elevation was a token that the Messiah of David's line would indeed come – and it is a matter of incidental interest that Zerubbabel the son of Shealtiel figures among the ancestors of Jesus in both the Gospel genealogies.[1]

The word Messiah (Hebrew *māshiaḥ*) is a verbal adjective with passive force from the Hebrew verb *māshaḥ* ("anoint"); the Messiah is thus the "Anointed One" – not merely with reference to a past act of anointing but to the sacred character and power which he possesses in consequence of that act. The corresponding Greek word is the verbal adjective of *chriō* ("I anoint") – *christos*, whence the English form "Christ". But in the Old Testament the title Messiah is not applied distinctively to the coming deliverer of David's line as it is in later Jewish and Christian literature. When the term "Messiah" occurs in the Old Testament, it is normally defined by some qualifying addition, such as "the Messiah of Yahweh" or "my Messiah". "This," as Geerhardus Vos points out, "is of some importance because it shows that the name had not yet been petrified into a conventional designation, but was a phrase the force of whose original conception was still being felt."[2]

Nor was it only of kings that the term was used; the high priest, for example, is called "the anointed priest",[3] because he was consecrated with oil. The "anointed one" in Daniel's oracle of the seventy heptads is best understood in a priestly sense.[4] A prophet might also be anointed for his sacred service, as Elisha was,[5] but not so regularly as the king and the high priest; so the term "Messiah" is not applied in the Old Testament to a prophet as such (apart from Psalm 105:15, where "anointed ones" and "prophets" stand in synonymous parallelism).

After Zerubbabel, the descendants of David pass into obscurity. The king who comes to Zion "triumphant and victorious" in Zechariah 9:9 (an oracle of uncertain date), "humble and riding on an ass",[6] is almost certainly envisaged as belonging to the Davidic dynasty, if one may judge from the earlier associations of the language used of him:

> his dominion shall be from the sea to sea,
> and from the River to the ends of the earth.[7]

Throughout the centuries of Persian and Graeco-Macedonian supremacy, and in the brief spell of national independence under the

---

[1] Matt. 1:12 f.; Luke 3:27 (where "Rhesa" is probably not an independent name but Zerubbabel's title "prince", Aram. *rēshā*); this coincidence is the more striking as the two genealogies are otherwise completely divergent between David and Joseph, the husband of Mary.
[2] G. Vos, *The Self-Disclosure of Jesus* (Grand Rapids, 1954), p. 105.
[3] Lev. 4:3, 5, 16; 6:22 (Heb. *kōhēn māshīaḥ*).
[4] Dan. 9:25 (Jeshua?), 26 (Onias III?).
[5] I Kings 19:16. [6] See pp. 49, 106 f.
[7] Zech. 9:10b, echoing Psalm 72:8.

> The sceptre shall not depart from Judah,
> nor the ruler's staff from between his feet,
> until he comes to whom it belongs;
> and to him shall be the obedience of the peoples.[1]

It might have been thought at one time that the establishment of the Davidic monarchy exhausted the terms of the promise in Judah's blessing; again, with the fall of that monarchy it might have been thought that the promise had been annulled. But Ezekiel declares that the prophecy neither found its ultimate fulfilment in the rise of David's house nor met its final frustration in the ruin of that house. Another David, a true shepherd to Israel, is yet to come,[2] the one to whom the sovereignty belongs by right, and in him all the promises made to Judah's tribe and David's house will be perfectly satisfied.

3. Hope Deferred

When at last the edict came which authorized the return of the exiles and the rebuilding of the temple at Jerusalem, it was natural that a restoration of David's dynasty should be looked for at the same time. And indeed, the restored community was administered at first by governors belonging to the house of David, appointed by the Persian authorities. It may be that some pinned their hopes to Sheshbazzar or Zerubbabel[3] as the restorer of David's dominion. Whereas one of Jeremiah's oracles assures Jehoiachin, last king of Judah but one, that even if he were the signet-ring on Yahweh's right hand he would be torn off and thrown away,[4] that king's grandson, Zerubbabel, is acclaimed in an oracle of the post-exilic prophet Haggai as destined to occupy the position of Yahweh's signet-ring which his ancestor had forfeited.[5] But Zerubbabel did not prove to be the second David of whom Jeremiah and Ezekiel spoke. In one of Zechariah's visions he is hailed as the "Branch" or scion of David's house; as builder of the second temple he "shall bear royal honour, and shall sit and rule upon his throne", while by his throne stands his high-priestly colleague Jeshua (grandson of the last chief priest in the first temple), "and peaceful understanding shall be between them both".[6] It may even be that Zerubbabel and Jeshua are the "two anointed" (literally "sons of oil") who, in another of Zechariah's visions, "stand by the Lord of the whole earth"[7] and thus provide a model for the two witnesses of the New Testament Apocalypse.[8] The fact that, after the return from captivity, a prince of the house of David was governor of Judah showed at least that the promise of "a

---

[1] Gen. 49:10, quoted at Qumran (4Q *Patriarchal Blessings*, lines 1 ff.) as an oracle pointing to "the rightful Messiah, the Branch (Heb. ṣemaḥ, 'shoot' or 'scion', as in Jer. 23:5; 33:15; Zech. 3:8; 6:12) of David". See also p. 76, n. 12.
[2] Ezek. 34:23 f.; 37:24 f.   [3] Cf. Ezra 1:8, 10; 3:2, 8; 4:2 f.   [4] Jer. 22:24 f.
[5] Haggai 2:23.   [6] Zech. 3:8; 6:12 f.   [7] Zech. 4:14.   [8] Rev. 11:4.

a great king of that line – Immanuel, the Virgin's Son, the Prince of the Four Names, on whom the Spirit of Yahweh would rest in unprecedented fulness, whose everlasting kingdom would be marked by righteousness and peace.[1] The fulfilment of all this was assured by "the zeal of Yahweh of hosts"[2] – His loving care for His people and for the honour of His own pledged word. And Isaiah's contemporary Micah looks to David's town of Bethlehem for the promised deliverer and ruler of Israel, the man whose advent establishes peace, the shepherd-king who will be "great to the ends of the earth."[3]

The events of the immediate future, however, showed no sign of the fulfilment of these hopes. The recession of Assyrian power gave Judah and Jerusalem a respite of a century or so, but the day came when the southern monarchy, too, was abolished, and Zedekiah, the last king of David's line, was carried into exile. The fragment of Israelite territory which had remained to David's dynasty became a minor province of the Babylonian Empire. Where now were "the holy and sure blessings of David"?

Even now, when the gloom was thickest, a gleam of promise shone. Jeremiah assured his people that, in place of the unworthy rulers who occupied David's throne in the closing days of the monarchy, God would raise up a righteous scion of the royal house, a second and greater David; "and he shall reign as king and deal wisely, and execute justice and righteousness in the land. In his days Judah will be saved, and Israel will dwell securely. And this is the name by which he will be called, 'Yahweh is our righteousness'."[4] The last king of Judah, Zedekiah ($Ṣidqi$-$yāhū$) had proved untrue to the meaning of his name, "Yahweh's righteousness"; but another would rise who would rightly bear the name $Yahweh$-$ṣidqēnū$. To those who feared that the promises of God had been proved ineffective, His reply was: "If you can break my covenant with the day, and my covenant with the night, so that day and night will not come at their appointed time, then also my covenant with David my servant may be broken, so that he shall not have a son to reign on this throne".[5]

Similarly Jeremiah's younger contemporary Ezekiel, contemplating the downfall of the perjured Zedekiah, sees that the crown of David will remain without a wearer for long, but not for ever: in due course one who is worthy to wear it will come and receive it. "A ruin, ruin, ruin I will make it; there shall not be even a trace of it until he comes whose right it is; and to him I will give it."[6] These words echo a promise which was ancient even in Ezekiel's day, the words spoken of Judah in the Blessing of Jacob:

---

[1] Isa. 7:14; 9:6 f.; 11:1 ff.;32:1 ff.   [2] Isa. 9:7b.
[3] Micah 5:2 ff.   [4] Jer. 23:5 f.; cf. 33:15 f.
[5] Jer. 33:20 f.; cf. verses 25 f. The promise to the house of David is accompanied by a similar promise to the house of Levi, which is not taken up in the New Testament (see p. 72, n. 1).
[6] Ezek. 21:27.

High;¹ and made it not only the capital of his kingdom but also the central sanctuary of the nation by enshrining the ark of the covenant there. At the enshrinement of the ark he exercised priestly functions,² and as he had the gift of prophecy as well,³ he was one of the few figures in Israel's history in whom the three offices of prophet, priest and king concurred. He led his people to victory against the surrounding nations and built up an empire stretching, by direct or indirect control, from the frontier of Egypt to the upper Euphrates. When he bequeathed this empire to his son Solomon, it might have appeared that the glories promised to David and his house had reached their peak.

But as Solomon's reign advanced, the lustre began to fade. One subject-nation after another regained its independence, and on Solomon's death the kingdom of Israel itself split into two parts; and the southern monarchy, which remained with the house of David, was the smaller and poorer of the two.

Worse was to follow. A time came, about two hundred years after Solomon's death, when the northern monarchy was incorporated in the Assyrian Empire, and even the house of David was threatened with extinction. But in these years of darkness the covenant mercies promised to David were confirmed afresh. An oracle appended to the words of Amos looks forward to the restoration of the imperial glories of the dynasty:

> "In that day I will raise up
> the booth of David that is fallen
> and repair its breaches,
> and raise up its ruins,
> and rebuild it as in the days of old;
> that they may possess the remnant of Edom
> and all the nations who are called by my name,"
> says Yahweh who does this.⁴

The remnant of Edom and all the nations that are called by Yahweh's name are those that paid tribute to David at the widest extent of his power; the day will come, says the oracle, when they will once more be tributary to the house of David.

Even Hosea, a prophet of the northern kingdom, declared that, after a long captivity, the children of Israel would return and seek Yahweh their God and David their king: their enjoyment of Yahweh's "goodness in the latter days" would be conjoined with the renewal of their allegiance to the line of David.⁵ In the southern kingdom Isaiah announced that greater glories awaited the house of David than any it had known thus far, under

---

¹ This, and not the promises made to the tribe of Levi or the house of Zadok (Jer. 33:18, 21b, 22b; Ezek. 44:15 ff.), is the event on which (via the oracle of Psalm 110:4) is based the New Testament exposition of the priesthood of Jesus (Heb. 5:6, etc.).
² II Sam. 6:14 ff.; cf. 8:18b.   ³ II Sam. 23:1 f.; cf. Acts 2:30.
⁴ Amos 9:11 f.; see p. 79 with n. 3.   ⁵ Hosea 3:4 f.

THE SON OF DAVID

> Her priests I will clothe with salvation,
>   and her saints will shout for joy.
> There I will make a horn to sprout for David;
>   I have prepared a lamp for my anointed.
> His enemies I will clothe with shame,
>   but upon himself his crown will shed its lustre."[1]

In another psalm these promises are recalled, in a day when the fortunes of David's house were at a low ebb, as "Yahweh's steadfast love"[2] (*ḥeseḏ* in the plural, as in Isaiah 55:3), and they are spelt out in these terms:

> I have found David, my servant;
>   with my holy oil I have anointed him;
> so that my hand shall ever abide with him,
>   my arm also shall strengthen him . . .
> My faithfulness and my steadfast love shall be with him,
>   and in my name shall his horn be exalted.
> I will set his hand on the sea
>   and his right hand on the rivers.
> He shall cry to me, "Thou art my Father,
>   my God, and the Rock of my salvation."
> And I will make him the first-born,
>   the highest of the kings of the earth.
> My steadfast love I will keep for him for ever,
>   and my covenant will stand firm for him.
> I will establish his line for ever
>   and his throne as the days of the heavens . . .
> I will not violate my covenant,
>   or alter the word that went forth from my lips.
> Once for all I have sworn by my holiness;
>   I will not lie to David.
> His line shall endure for ever,
>   his throne as long as the sun before me.
> Like the moon it shall be established for ever;
>   it shall stand firm while the skies endure.[3]

In these and other psalms[4] it is emphasized that Yahweh's oath to David is inviolable; His mercies are eternal; His covenant is sure.

2. David's Fallen Booth

David was not only the founder of a great dynasty. Rising to power in a day of disaster for Israel, he enabled the united tribes to throw off the yoke of their oppressors, the Philistines and others. He occupied the fortress of Jerusalem, seat of the ancient royalty of Melchizedek, priest of God Most

---
[1] Psalm 132:11–18.   [2] Psalm 89:1.
[3] Psalm 89:20–37. The word "highest" in verse 27 (quoted in Rev. 1:5) is *'elyōn*, found first as a divine title in the Melchizedek narrative of Gen. 14:18 ff.
[4] Cf. Psalm 72.

"I will make an everlasting covenant with you", says Yahweh to His people whom He is about to bring back from exile, "my steadfast, sure love for David."[1] The group of prophetic oracles to which this promise belongs (Isaiah 40-55) opens with the message of consolation which foretells the end of Jerusalem's desolations and the return of her deported citizens from the lands of their banishment to their ancestral home. This restoration is to be the victorious achievement of Israel's God: to accomplish it He is overruling the course of international history.

This is the background against which God assures His people that, despite the diminished state of their fortunes, He has not forgotten the promises which He made in earlier days to their great king, David. He reaffirms these promises; He will surely fulfil them. Even an ordinary promise of God is certain of fulfilment, but the promises made to David are more than ordinary promises. They were given in a form which David himself describes as "an everlasting covenant, ordered in all things, and secure".[2] They were communicated by the mouth of the prophet Nathan:

> I will appoint a place for my people Israel, and will plant them, that they may dwell in their own place, and be disturbed no more ... Moreover Yahweh declares to you that Yahweh will make you a house. When your days are fulfilled and you lie down with your fathers, I will raise up your offspring after you, who shall come forth from your body, and I will establish his kingdom. He shall build a house for my name, and I will establish the throne of his kingdom for ever. I will be his father, and he shall be my son. ... And your house and your kingdom shall be made sure for ever before me; your throne shall be established for ever.

These promises, expressed thus in prose form in II Samuel 7:10-16, were probably couched originally in poetic form, of which we may catch echoes here and there in the Psalter. In Psalm 132, for example, the divine oath to David is conjoined with a similar one regarding David's capital city:

> Yahweh swore to David a sure oath
> from which he will not turn back:
> "One of the sons of your body
> I will set on your throne.
> If your sons keep the covenant
> and my testimonies which I shall teach them,
> their sons also for ever
> shall sit upon your throne."
> For Yahweh has chosen Zion;
> he has desired it for his habitation:
> "This is my resting place for ever;
> here I will dwell, for I have desired it.
> I will abundantly bless her provisions;
> I will satisfy her poor with bread.

---

[1] Isa. 55:3.   [2] II Sam. 23:5.

> With upright heart he tended them,
> and guided them with skilful hand.[1]

Moreover, the place which the Davidic dynasty occupied in the national cult – to judge by many of the psalms – suggests that its establishment and the covenant-promises associated with it did gain entrance to Israel's *credenda*.

We have seen already[2] how Paul's synagogue-sermon at Pisidian Antioch, after surveying (like the psalm quoted above) the sequence of mighty acts accomplished by "the God of this people" from the Exodus to the establishment of the Davidic monarchy, goes straight on from David to "great David's greater Son", in whom he proclaims the true fulfilment of the promises made to David.

> We bring you the good news that what God promised to the fathers, this he has fulfilled to us their children by raising Jesus; as also it is written in the second psalm,
>
> > "Thou art my Son,
> > today I have begotten thee".
>
> And as for the fact that he raised him from the dead, no more to return to corruption, he spoke in this way,
>
> > "I will give you the holy and sure blessings of David."
>
> Therefore he says also in another psalm,
>
> > "Thou wilt not let thy Holy One see corruption".
>
> For David, after he had served the counsel of God in his own generation, fell asleep, and was laid with his fathers, and saw corruption; but he whom God raised up saw no corruption.[3]

The "holy and sure blessings of David" are the steadfast, reliable covenant-mercies which Yahweh confirmed to David and his house. The Greek text of Paul's sermon reproduces the Septuagint reading of Isaiah 55:3, in which *ta hosia* ("the holy things")[4] may presuppose a vocalization *ḥăsīdē* (construct plural of *ḥāsīd*) instead of *ḥasdē* (construct plural of *ḥesed*) which appears in the Massoretic text. The distinction is not a great one: *ḥesed*, traditionally rendered "loving kindness", expresses the attitude which God takes towards those to whom He has pledged Himself in solemn covenant, and which He expects them to show to Him and to one another; *ḥāsīd* is a cognate adjective describing persons or objects involved in such a covenant relationship.

---

[1] Psalm 78:67–72. Yahweh's choice of David as His anointed and of Zion as His sanctuary are twin themes (cf. the extract from Psalm 132, pp. 70 f. below).
[2] See p. 37.   [3] Acts 13:32–7.
[4] In the sermon there is a link between the ὅσια ("holy things") of this quotation and the ὅσιος ("holy one") of Psalm 16:10 quoted immediately afterwards as a *testimonium* of Christ's resurrection (as also in Acts 2:25 ff.).

CHAPTER VI

THE SON OF DAVID

*"Great triumphs he gives to his king
and shows steadfast love to his anointed,
to David and his descendants for ever."*

1. *The Promise to David*

IN THE BIBLICAL PRESENTATION OF EACH OF THE THEMES WHICH WE HAVE surveyed thus far there is one aspect at which we have looked only in passing, if at all. If the theology of the New Testament writers has been influenced by the divine covenants made with Abraham and later with his descendants in Moses' day, it has been manifestly influenced also by the covenant which Yahweh established with David and his house.[1]

Professor von Rad holds that the record of David did not gain admission to the history of salvation in the proper sense of that phrase because it is not included in the early credal acknowledgements. "That Jahweh had led Israel out of Egypt was a part of Israel's confession at all times. But that he had guaranteed the continuance of the throne of David ... was never taken up into the series of these confessional statements."[2] But – while the promises to David and his posterity could not find a place in premonarchical statements, in later expansions of the confessional recital of Yahweh's dealings with Israel the establishment of the throne of David[3] is the goal to which His earlier dealings with Israel led up. So Psalm 78, after a review of His dealings with His people from Egypt onwards, ends in these terms:

> He rejected the tent of Joseph,
>   he did not choose the tribe of Ephraim;
> but he chose the tribe of Judah,
>   Mount Zion, which he loves.
> He built his sanctuary like the high heavens,
>   like the earth, which he has founded for ever.
> He chose David his servant,
>   and took him from the sheepfolds;
> from tending the ewes that had young he brought him
>   to be the shepherd of Jacob his people,
>   of Israel his inheritance.

---

[1] II Sam. 23:5; Psalms 89:3 f., 28, 34; 132:12.
[2] G. von Rad, *Old Testament Theology* i (Edinburgh, 1962), p. 306.
[3] Cf. A. G. Hebert, *The Throne of David* (London, 1941).

covenant-loyalty to Him: Lo-ruhamah (not the object of my compassion or mercy) and Lo-ammi (not my people).¹ But for old time's sake Yahweh will not allow this broken relationship to remain so for ever; He looks forward to the time when those who at present are not His people will once more be His people, and when those who at present have no claim on His kindly feelings will once more be the objects of His mercy. "In the place where it was said to them 'You are not my people', it shall be said to them, 'Sons of the living God'.... And I will have pity on Lo-ruhamah, and to Lo-ammi I will say, 'You are my people'; and he shall say, 'Thou art my God'."²

In I Peter 2:10 (as in Romans 9:25 f.) this promise, which originally referred to a situation within the national frontiers of Israel, is seen to embody a principle which in apostolic days was being worked out on a world-wide scale. Great numbers of Gentiles, who had never been the people of God – who, in the language of the Deuteronomic Song of Moses, had formerly been a "no-people"³ – and had no claim on His covenant mercy, were coming to be enrolled among His people and to be the recipients of His mercy. The scale of the action was far wider than in Hosea's day, but the same pattern was recognizable. Through the Gentile mission, in lands where the people of God had once been unrepresented, there were now many believers whom the living God acknowledged as His sons. An exposition like that of I Peter 2:1–10 was well calculated to impress recent converts from paganism with a sense of the nobility of that heritage of grace and glory into which they had entered by faith in Christ.

---

¹ Hosea 1:6–9.
² Hosea 1:10b; 2:23.
³ Heb. *lō 'am* (Deut. 32:21, quoted in Rom. 10:19).

inquisition into the healing of the lame man in the temple court, assures the court that the healing was effected "by the name of Jesus Christ of Nazareth" and adds: "This is the stone which was rejected by you builders, but which has become the head of the corner."

The second *testimonium* which relates to unbelievers is Isaiah 8:14 f. (a passage which is thoroughly conflated with Isaiah 28:16 by Paul in Romans 9:32 f. to provide a composite *testimonium* of Israel's refusal of the gospel). There the prophet foretells how the Assyrian invasion will sweep over the land of Israel – "Immanuel's land" – like the waters of a great flood. But there will be one place of refuge from the overwhelming flood: the God of Israel will Himself prove to be "a sanctuary" to all who put their trust in Him, a rock on which they will find a secure footing. Those who refuse to trust Him, however, relying instead on other powers, will be swept by the flood against this rock and come to grief upon it; to them, far from being a place of refuge, it will prove a dangerous obstacle – "a stone of offence and a rock of stumbling to both houses of Israel, a trap and a snare to the inhabitants of Jerusalem; and many shall stumble thereon; they shall fall and be broken; they shall be snared and taken." So, in Luke's account of the parable of the vineyard, Jesus brings this oracle into relation with "the stone which the builders rejected", saying, "every one who falls on that stone will be broken to pieces".[1] It is one of many arguments in support of Professor Dodd's thesis about the New Testament use of complete contexts from the Old Testament that in the next chapter of I Peter the words which immediately precede this Isaianic *testimonium* ("But Yahweh of hosts, him you shall sanctify; let him be your fear and let him be your dread") are applied in a modified form to Christians called to account, and perhaps to suffering, for the hope that is in them by hostile authorities: "Have no fear of them, nor be troubled, but in your hearts sanctify Christ as Lord."[2]

(*d*) Another set of oracles adduced at the end of this opening section of I Peter 2 is drawn from the prophecy of Hosea, and the fact that the same oracles are used in the same sense by Paul in Romans 9:25 f. attests the antiquity of this Christian application of Hosea's prophecy.

Hosea was taught to see in his own domestic tragedy something of Yahweh's dealings with His people Israel. When he took Gomer as his wife and she in due course gave birth to a son, he acknowledged the child as his and called him Jezreel ("God's sowing").[3] But her second and third children, he was convinced, were not his, and he gave them names which expressed his disillusionment: Lo-ruhamah (one for whom no natural affection or compassion is felt) and Lo-ammi (no kin of mine). These names also betokened Yahweh's attitude to Israel, because Israel had broken her

[1] Luke 20:17 f., where this stone-oracle (with that of Psalm 118:22) is conflated with the stone of Nebuchadnezzar's dream (Dan. 2:31 ff.); cf. p. 26 above.
[2] I Peter 3:14 f., adapting Isa. 8:12 f.
[3] Hosea 1:3 f.

Divine election, as we have seen, is not merely an individual concern; it means incorporation into God's chosen people, those whom He has reserved for Himself to manifest His glory in the world both by word and by action.

(c) The unitive exegesis of a group of "stone" oracles appears in so many strata of the New Testament that it must be recognized as unusually primitive: in the Synoptic tradition it is given a setting in the ministry of Jesus. In I Peter 2:5-8 three of these oracles are treated in this way.

One of them is Isaiah 28:16, where, in the course of a warning about the impending deluge of Assyrian invasion which will sweep away the "refuge of lies" in which the king and people of Judah are putting their trust, the word of God comes to the prophet:

> Behold, I am laying in Zion for a foundation
> a stone, a tested stone,
> a precious cornerstone, of a sure foundation:
> "He who believes will not be in haste".

The last clause (perhaps to be rendered "He who believes will not panic") is evidently the motto inscribed on this foundation stone. The stone is the righteous remnant of the people of God, the hope of the future, which in other oracles of Isaiah is embodied in the promised prince of the house of David. It is viewed not only as a foundation stone but as a cornerstone – the stone cut out beforehand, which both bonds the structure together and serves as a "stone of testing" to show whether the building has been carried out to the architect's specifications. This figure is used also in Ephesians 2:20, where "Christ Jesus himself" is "the cornerstone in whom the whole structure [of His people's corporate life] is joined together and grows into a holy temple in the Lord."

In so far as this is called "a *precious* cornerstone", says Peter, this is a feature of it which is appreciated by you who believe;[1] as for unbelievers, other features of the stone are more applicable to them and these are mentioned in two other *testimonia*:

The first of these is Psalm 118:22 f.:

> The stone which the builders rejected
> has become the head of the corner.
> This is Yahweh's doing;
> it is marvellous in our eyes.

This *testimonium* is used by Jesus in Mark 12:10 f., to drive home the point of the parable of the vineyard to hearers who "perceived that he had told the parable against them". Its application is made even more explicit in Acts 4:11 where Peter, standing with John to reply to the Sanhedrin's

---

[1] I Peter 2:7a. On the cornerstone of Scripture see S. H. Hooke, *The Siege Perilous* (London, 1956), pp. 235 ff.

here for the people of God: they are "a chosen race, a royal priesthood, a holy nation, God's own people".[1]

On Mount Sinai Moses received this message from Yahweh for the people of Israel: "You have seen what I did to the Egyptians, and how I bore you on eagles' wings and brought you to myself. Now therefore, if you will obey my voice and keep my covenant, you shall be *my own possession* among all peoples; for all the earth is mine, and you shall be to me *a kingdom of priests* and *a holy nation*."[2] The three italicized phrases are echoed, if not explicitly quoted, in I Peter 2:9. Like Israel, the believing community of the New Testament is a nation set apart by God for Himself, chosen to be peculiarly His own, called to exercise a royal priesthood. The royal priesthood of Christians seems to have been a widespread concept by the end of the apostolic age, as is suggested by its being incorporated without explanation in the doxologies of Revelation 1:6 and 5:10. Those who shared their Priest-King's humiliation and suffering knew themselves called to share His intercession and sovereignty, but the background of the wording in the apocalyptic doxologies as in I Peter is to be found in Exodus 19:6.

The priestly character of the new community is mentioned also in I Peter 2:5, where it is described as "a holy priesthood to offer up spiritual sacrifices acceptable to God through Jesus Christ" – priesthood and temple in one, for this is a temple of living stones or, if the language of Ephesians be borrowed again, "a dwelling place of God in the Spirit".[3] What the "spiritual sacrifices" might be is suggested by other New Testament writers whose thought moves along parallel lines: Paul appeals to the Christians of Rome to present their "bodies as a living sacrifice, holy and acceptable to God", which is their "spiritual worship", and to have their minds renewed so that mind and life alike may be brought into conformity with the will of God.[4] The writer to the Hebrews exhorts his readers to "offer up a sacrifice of praise to God, ... the fruit of lips that acknowledge his name" (words which themselves are taken from Hosea's call to Israel to ask God to accept "the fruit of our lips" instead of animal sacrifices),[5] while he reminds them that doing good and sharing what they have with others are also "sacrifices ... pleasing to God".[6]

Another Old Testament scripture from which designations for the new community are drawn in I Peter 2:9 is Isaiah 43:20 f., where the God of Israel speaks of "my chosen people, the people whom I formed for myself, that they might declare my praise". So Peter tells these Gentile recruits to the Christian fellowship that it is their function to "declare the wonderful deeds of him who called you out of darkness into his marvellous light".

---

[1] I Peter 2:9a. Cf. the similar passage in Titus 2:14 ("a people of his own"), based on Ex. 19:5; Deut. 14:2.
[2] Ex. 19:4–6.   [3] Eph. 2:22.   [4] Rom. 12:1 f.
[5] Heb. 13:15, with an allusion to Hosea 14:2.
[6] Heb. 13:16.

to recent converts to Christianity who were "now" passing through the antitypical water.¹ They are described as newly-born infants, "born anew ... through the living and abiding word of God".² They are urged to acquire an appetite for unadulterated spiritual milk, so that they may grow up to health of soul³ – there is no word here of the "strong meat" or "solid food" which other New Testament writers recommend for those of greater maturity.⁴ They are joining a new community, a new race, a new family, and they must follow the way of life which their new association demands. Their conduct must be transformed: they must "put off" the old practices and "put on" a new character. This transformation was symbolized in the early church, though perhaps not so early as this, in the discarding of former garments and the putting on of new ones on emerging from the baptismal font.

These lessons are reinforced by the application of a number of Old Testament passages, of which those quoted in I Peter 2:1–10 deserve special attention. They fall into four groups:

(a) the baptismal use of Psalm 34 (verses 3, 4a);
(b) a collection of Old Testament designations for the people of God (verses 5, 9);
(c) a collection of Old Testament "stone" oracles (verses 4b, 6–8);
(d) the message of Hosea applied to the Gentile mission (verse 10).

(a) There is good reason to believe that from early days Psalm 34 was regularly used in the church's liturgy.⁵ In I Peter 3:10–12 a considerable section of this psalm is quoted by way of ethical paraenesis;⁶ but its wording has left traces in the opening paragraph of the second chapter with which we are more particularly concerned at present. The words "you have tasted the kindness of the Lord" are drawn from Psalm 34:8a ("O taste and see that Yahweh is good!") and the invitation which immediately follows, "Come to him ...", may be designed to echo Psalm 34:5 where, in place of the Massoretic text which is translated "Look to him and be radiant" in RSV, the Septuagint rendering is "Come to him and be enlightened" – which may in turn explain the use of the term "enlightenment" as a synonym for baptism in early Christianity.⁷

(b) More instructive are the various Old Testament designations used

---

¹ For "now" see I Peter 3:21; for the view that I Peter 1:3–4:11 has the form of a baptismal homily see R. Perdelwitz, *Die Mysterienreligionen und das Problem des I Petrusbriefes* (Giessen, 1911); B. H. Streeter, *The Primitive Church* (London, 1929), pp. 115 ff.; also R. P. Martin, "The Composition of I Peter in Recent Study", *Vox Evangelica* I (1962), pp. 29 ff.
² I Peter 1:23.   ³ I Peter 2:2.   ⁴ Cf. I Cor. 3:2; Heb. 5:12–14.
⁵ *Apostolic Constitutions* viii. 13; Cyril of Jerusalem, *Mystagogical Catecheses* v. 17; Jerome, *Epistle* 28.
⁶ Psalm 34:12–16.
⁷ Cf. Justin, *Apology* I. 61. 12 f.; 65. 1; perhaps also Heb. 6:4; 10:32 (where the Syriac Peshitta renders "enlightened" by "baptized"); a possible explanation of this usage is suggested by Eph. 5:14.

c

subject of God's election, to be His "chosen instrument" to carry His name to others that they too may hear the quickening sound. When Paul was spoken of in these terms, "I will show him", added the risen Lord, "how much he must suffer for the sake of my name."[1]

4. The New Israel

When Jesus chose the Twelve, their number implied that they represented the faithful remnant of the old Israel who would also be the foundation of the new. This is not a matter of speculation; it comes to clear enough expression in the primitive logion which promises them that in the new age they will be enthroned along with their Master, "judging the twelve tribes of Israel".[2] When the crucial test came, the faithful remnant was reduced to one person, the Son of Man who entered death single-handed and rose again as his people's representative. With him the people of God died and rose again: hence the New Testament people of God, while preserving its continuity with the Old Testament people of God, is at the same time a new creation. This pattern of death and resurrection is sacramentally set forth in baptism, in which the heirs of the new creation are identified with the Christ who died and rose again – which brings us to another document which presents the New Testament teaching about the people of God in terms of the Old Testament background.

The First Epistle of Peter is addressed to people called "the exiles of the Dispersion" in five provinces of Asia Minor, who are further described as "chosen and destined by God the Father and sanctified by the Spirit for obedience to Jesus Christ and for sprinkling with his blood".[3] In these expressions terms earlier applied to Israel are applied to Christian communities, their new connotation being made clear by the distinctively Christian terms with which they are amplified. The frontiers of the people of God are now more extensive than they had been before Christ came: in the language of the Epistle to the Ephesians (with which I Peter has close affinities) membership in the beloved community is now open on equal terms of grace to those who were formerly "alienated from the commonwealth of Israel, and strangers to the covenants of promise" by which God bound His people to Himself in earlier days. Now believing Gentiles are "no longer strangers and sojourners, but . . . fellow citizens with the [original] saints and members of the household of God",[4] and it is to such believing Gentiles that I Peter is directed.

Without examining in detail questions introductory to the study of this epistle, let me say that I am disposed to accept the view that in I Peter 1:3–4:11 we may recognize a baptismal homily in written form addressed

[1] Acts 9:15 f.
[2] Matt. 19:28; Luke 22:30.
[3] I Peter 1:1 f.
[4] Eph. 2:12, 19.

the joyful news of God's salvation which they have received through their Master's death and resurrection.[1]

For Israel was not chosen that the other nations might be consigned to perdition, but that through Israel's election they might all enjoy God's blessing. So when God called Abraham, the first subject of divine election in the biblical record, He promised not only to bless him but to make him a blessing to others, and if the words "by you all the families of the earth will bless themselves"[2] originally meant that Abraham's prosperity would constitute the standard by which others would measure theirs (saying "May I be as blessed as Abraham"), in the course of the biblical revelation they acquired a profounder meaning: the blessing which Abraham received by faith comes to all who like him believe God.[3] This insistence pervades the New Testament: if some are "the chosen few" it does not follow that "all others will be damned". In the parable of the sheep and the goats those to whom the Son of Man says, "Come, O blessed of my Father", are clearly distinguished from the inner circle designated as "these my brethren".[4] Similarly, in the apocalyptic vision of the New Jerusalem, the beloved community which is portrayed under the guise of this heavenly city is a blessing to the new earth: "By its light shall the nations walk."[5] Because the light of the divine presence irradiates this commonwealth of the elect, the proclamation goes out from the heavenly throne in the ancient covenant language: "Behold the dwelling of God is with men. He will dwell with them, and they shall be his peoples."[6]

One final point about Israel's special election: it involved not only special service but special suffering, and the one in whom Israel's mission was fulfilled, the one who in a unique degree is the Elect One of God – "my chosen, in whom my soul delights"[7] – was not exempt from suffering because God delighted in him. On the contrary, it was by suffering that the Servant of Yahweh accomplished the ministry entrusted to him; it was because he gave up his life as a sin-offering that Yahweh's purpose prospered in his hand.[8] So, in the New Testament those who are called and chosen to enter into the ministry of the Servant cannot discharge the commission laid upon them unless, like Paul, they know something of "the fellowship of his sufferings" or are prepared to "complete what is lacking in Christ's afflictions".[9] It is a glorious thing, but a costly thing, to be the

---

[1] Luke 24:46-8; Acts 1:8 (echoing Isa. 43:10, 12; 44:8).
[2] Gen. 12:3; cf. 18:18; 22:18; 26:4; 28:14.
[3] Cf. Rom. 4:3, 22 ff.; Gal. 3:6, quoting Gen. 15:6; Gal. 3:9 (see p. 52), following the quotation of Gen. 18:18 in verse 8. Quite apart from the Christian fulfilment, Gentiles who become proselytes to the Jewish faith and way of life have, from Old Testament times onwards, entered into the covenant with Abraham and "taken refuge under the wings of the God of Israel" (Ruth 2:12).
[4] Matt. 25:34, 40.   [5] Rev. 21:24.
[6] Rev. 21:3. The plural "peoples" is more likely to be original than the variant "people"; the singular is probably the result of accommodation to the Old Testament text.
[7] Isa. 42:1.   [8] See pp. 87, 96.   [9] Phil. 3:10; Col. 1:24.

as Yahweh's chosen people were so great, their responsibilities were proportionately great; wickedness in Israel was dealt with more severely than wickedness in other nations, because Israel had better opportunities of knowing what was right:

> You only have I known
> of all the families of the earth;
> therefore I will punish you
> for all your iniquities.[1]

This was a hard lesson to learn. As late as the close of the pre-Christian era we find the author of the book of Wisdom arguing that, while God afflicts the Gentiles in pure retribution, the same afflictions are remedial in intention when they fall on the Israelites:

> For thou didst test them as a father does in warning,
> but thou didst examine the ungodly as a stern king does in condemnation ...
> So while chastening us thou scourgest our enemies ten thousand times more,
> so that we may meditate upon thy goodness when we judge,
> and when we are judged we may expect mercy[2]

– an attitude which Paul refutes in the Epistle to the Romans, when he assures the Jew who condemns Gentile immorality that if he does not make use of the opportunity of repentance afforded him by the kindness of God he is storing up wrath for himself against the day when God's righteous judgement is to be revealed.[3]

Again, in the Old Testament Israel is not chosen to enjoy the knowledge of God in selfish isolation, but to make that knowledge available to others. The people whom God brings back from exile are witnesses to all nations of God's delivering grace: Gentiles will acknowledge as they see what He has done for them:

> God is with you only, and there is no other,
> no god beside him.[4]

His saving work for Israel is a gospel proclamation to the world:

> Turn to me and be saved,
> all the ends of the earth!
> For I am God, and there is no other.
> By myself I have sworn,
> from my mouth has gone forth in righteousness
> a word that shall not return:
> "To me every knee shall bow,
> every tongue shall swear."[5]

The New Testament counterpart to this needs no emphasizing: the disciples of Christ are His witnesses, called to spread to the ends of the earth

---

[1] Amos 3:2. [2] Wisdom 11:10; 12:22. [3] Rom. 2:1–5.
[4] Isa. 45:14 (cf. I Cor. 14:25).
[5] Isa. 45:22 f. (cf. Rom. 14:11; Phil. 2:10 f.).

which guaranteed the fulfilment of God's promises to Israel. So long as there was a recognizable Israel, however small, in which these promises could be realized, there was no fear that they would come to nothing.

As Paul quotes the divine response to Elijah, so he quotes these Isaiah passages, and applies them to the same purpose: "Isaiah cries out concerning Israel: 'Though the number of the sons of Israel be as the sand of the sea, only a remnant of them will be saved; for the Lord will execute his sentence upon the earth with rigour and despatch.' And as Isaiah predicted,

> 'if the Lord of hosts had not left us a few survivors,
> we would have fared like Sodom
> and been made like Gomorrah'."[1]

"Only a remnant", but at least a remnant – "a remnant, chosen by grace".

3. The Chosen Race

This last phrase, "chosen by grace" – more literally in the older versions "according to the election of grace" (*kat' eklogēn charitos*) – relates to another biblical theme to which Paul pays special attention in Romans 9–11, the theme of divine election. Some traditional Christian expositions of this theme as it is presented in the New Testament have failed to take adequate account of its Old Testament background.[2]

In the Old Testament Israel is "chosen" by God "to be a people for his own possession, out of all the peoples that are on the face of the earth",[3] not for anything in Israel that merited His choice or rendered it peculiarly acceptable to Him, but because of His sheer grace.

> When Israel was a child, I loved him,
> and out of Egypt I called my son.[4]

But since He selected Israel for Himself, Israel must be a holy people: "You shall be holy, for I, Yahweh your God, am holy".[5] The same note is repeatedly struck in the New Testament: "As he who called you is holy, be holy yourselves in all your conduct; since it is written, 'You shall be holy, for I am holy'."[6]

The people of Israel were warned against supposing that they were God's favourites, for there was no partiality in Israel's God. If their privileges

---

[1] Rom. 9:27–9.
[2] Reference may be made to two outstanding studies of this subject: H. H. Rowley, *The Biblical Doctrine of Election* (London, 1950), and T. C. Vriezen, *Die Erwählung Israels nach dem Alten Testament* (Zürich, 1953).
[3] Deut. 7:6.
[4] Hosea 11:1. "God's eyes, passing the princes of the world, fell upon this slave boy, and He loved him and gave him a career" (G. A. Smith, *The Book of the Twelve Prophets*[2] i, London, 1928, p. 317).
[5] Lev. 11:44 f.; 19:2, etc.   [6] I Peter 1:15 f.

part to acknowledge Jesus as the Messiah, the one in whom the promises made to the fathers were fulfilled. True, he says, the majority of Israelites have not believed in Jesus, but that does not mean that God has rejected Israel. Some Israelites have believed (Paul mentions himself by way of example) and their belief guarantees the eventual regeneration of the people as a whole. As in Elijah's day God had his seven thousand, "so too at the present time there is a remnant, chosen by grace".[1]

In some of the great prophets of Israel this remnant theme is developed. The Assyrian conquests of the eighth century B.C., which obliterated the identity of so many small nations and city-states in South-West Asia, caused immense havoc in Israel too, but did not extinguish the name or memory of Israel. The surviving remnant might be small, but at least it was a remnant. Amos compares the impending destruction to the ravages of a lion among the flock, when a shepherd counts himself lucky if he can rescue "two legs, or a piece of an ear", as evidence of the sheep to which they once belonged.[2] One cannot place any hope in such miserable fragments; if there is to be any ground for hope, it must be in the sovereign act of God:

> it may be that Yahweh, the God of hosts,
> will be gracious to the remnant of Joseph.[3]

Isaiah's insistence on the remnant theme was so marked a feature of his preaching that it was reproduced in the name of one of his sons, Shear-jashub "a remnant will return".[4] At first this appears to have meant that *only* a remnant, the *merest* remnant, would survive the coming catastrophe and resume its former life:

> If Yahweh of hosts
> had not left us a few survivors,
> we should have been like Sodom,
> and become like Gomorrah.[5]

But as Isaiah's ministry continued, the remnant was seen not merely as one that would survive and return to its former home; it was seen as one that would return to God: "In that day the remnant of Israel and the survivors of the house of Jacob will no more lean upon him that smote them, but will lean upon Yahweh, the Holy One of Israel, in truth. A remnant will return, the remnant of Jacob, to the mighty God. For although your people Israel be as the sand of the sea, only a remnant of them will return."[6]

The "saved remnant" becomes the "saving remnant" – the remnant

---

[1] Rom. 11:1-5.
[2] Amos 3:12.
[3] Amos 5:15; "remnant" represents Heb. $sh^e\bar{e}rit$.
[4] Isa. 7:3. Cf. n. 6.
[5] Isa. 1:9.
[6] Isa. 10:20-22a; the clause $sh^e\bar{a}r\ y\bar{a}sh\underline{u}\underline{b}$ (the name of Isaiah's son), occurs twice over in this quotation. The title "Mighty God" ($\bar{e}l\ gibb\bar{o}r$) is one of those given to the "Prince of the Four Names" in Isa. 9:6.

unconvincing.¹ It is true that our author goes on to say that even the first *diathēkē* was ratified by blood – the blood of the covenant-victim – but the covenant-victim is not the *diathemenos*, whose death is necessary before the *diathēkē* can take effect. Indeed, it may be said that the reason Christ is surety as well as mediator of the new covenant is that He died to ensure its validity and efficacy. The first covenant had a mediator,² but no surety is mentioned in connexion with it. Christ is the surety of the new covenant because He is no mere covenant-victim but the *diathemenos*, the author of the *diathēkē*: His blood is "the blood of the covenant" by which His people are sanctified;³ His self-offering is so completely acceptable and effective that the covenant which it seals is an "eternal covenant",⁴ never to be superseded by another.

2. The Righteous Remnant

Within the empirical covenant community of Israel there was increasingly recognized to be a smaller group, who were in practice what the whole community was in theory, who took seriously the obligations of the covenant and endeavoured to carry them into effect. These are sometimes called the *ḥăsīḏīm*, the faithful, loyal or pious people of God. To them reference is made in one of the Asaphite psalms, where God commands:

> Gather to me my faithful ones
> who made a covenant with me by sacrifice!⁵

They are distinguished in this psalm from "the wicked", who also belong to the nation, for they recite God's statutes and take His covenant on their lips, but are told that their misconduct deprives them of all right to do so.⁶

This inner group of faithful souls is sometimes designated as a "remnant", those whom God reserves for Himself. Thus in the story of Elijah Yahweh replies to the prophet's complaint that all Israel apart from himself had forsaken the covenant with the assurance that there were many others who had maintained their loyalty and who would accordingly survive the wholesale slaughter which was coming as a judgement for the national apostasy: "Yet I will leave seven thousand in Israel, all the knees that have not bowed to Baal, and every mouth that has not kissed him."⁷

This precedent is invoked by Paul when he wrestles with the problem, present to his mind in an acute form because of the tension between his Jewish heritage and his Gentile apostleship, of Israel's failure for the most

---

¹ Cf. B. F. Westcott, *The Epistle to the Hebrews* (London, 1889), pp. 265 ff. The passive infinitive "be established" (φέρεσθαι) is probably used here in the technical sense "be registered" or "be produced as evidence".
² Cf. Gal. 3:19 f.   ³ Heb. 10:14, 29.   ⁴ Heb. 13:20.
⁵ Psalm 50:5.   ⁶ Psalm 50:16.
⁷ I Kings 19:18. "I will leave" represents Heb. *hish'arti*, from the same root as *shᵉ'ār*, *shᵉ'ērīṭ*, "remnant" (cf. p. 58, nn. 3, 6).

The explanation in Heb. 6:13 ff. of God's oath to Abraham[1] may be intended to apply also to the oath of Psalm 110:4, "Yahweh has sworn and will not change his mind, 'You are a priest for ever after the order of Melchizedek'." This oath, says the writer to the Hebrews, makes Jesus "the surety of a better covenant"[2] than that under which the priests of Aaron's line ministered, for they were not installed in office by such a solemnity as a divine oath. Moreover, the priestly ministry which Christ exercises "is as much more excellent than the old as the covenant he mediates is better, since it is enacted on better promises".[3] These "better promises" are those contained in the Jeremianic oracle of the new covenant, which is quoted *in extenso* in Heb. 8:8-12: the promises that God's laws will be written in His people's hearts, that they will all know Him, that He will pardon their iniquities, that He will remember their sins no more. Nothing like this was envisaged under the Mosaic covenant, says our author; on the contrary, the sacrificial ritual associated with that covenant made provision for the repeated remembrance of sins.[4] The announcement of a new covenant implies in itself that the previous one was defective (this may readily be inferred from the wording of Jeremiah's oracle) and the fact that the covenant so announced is a new one makes the previous one old in the sense of "obsolete".[5] Therefore, the argument proceeds, every institution established under the old covenant is likewise obsolete – sacrifice, sanctuary and priesthood. All have been replaced by something better – the perfect and unrepeatable self-offering of Christ, which purifies His people's conscience, removing from it the guilt which constituted the one effective barrier against their free access to God; the spiritual sanctuary, the communion of saints, in which they approach God to worship Him through Christ; the priestly ministry which Christ discharges for them perpetually in the presence of God.[6]

Of this new covenant Jesus is both surety and mediator.[7] The Epistle to the Hebrews confirms the sense of the eucharistic words of institution, in which the covenant is sealed by His blood, that is, His self-offering. In Heb. 9:15-17 this point is driven home through a play on the double meaning of *diathēkē* – covenant and testament. The death which redeems the people of God from their transgression of the terms of the first covenant and confirms to them "the promised eternal inheritance" is the death of Christ: "for where a *diathēkē* (testament) is involved, the death of the one who made it (*diathemenos*) must be established. For a *diathēkē* takes effect only at death, since it is not in force so long as the one who made it is alive." There is only one kind of *diathēkē* of which this is true: the attempts of Westcott and some others to keep the general sense of "covenant" throughout this passage and treat the death which "must be established" as the death of the covenant-victim are as unnecessary as they are

---

[1] See p. 53 above.   [2] Heb. 7:22.   [3] Heb. 8:6.   [4] Heb. 10:3.
[5] Heb. 8:13.   [6] Heb. 9:11-10:22.   [7] Heb. 8:6; 12:24.

THE PEOPLE OF GOD

them."[1] Of this new covenant Paul and his associates have been made ministers, and he rejoices that this ministry is not discharged under a written code which "kills" but "in the Spirit" who "gives life".[2] By contrast with the new covenant and its life-giving message, the law is described in terms of "the old covenant".[3] The law did indeed hold out life to those who kept it – "Do this and you shall live"[4] – but it pronounced a curse on those who broke it;[5] and since the law-breakers were always more numerous than the law-keepers, the general tendency of the old covenant was death.[6] The gospel, however, presents the way of life; through it the law-breaker who repents of his law-breaking finds forgiveness and justification by grace. Paul rejoices to be the administrator of a covenant which is life-giving and not death-dealing, a covenant which, far from imposing a yoke of bondage, conveys that freedom which rules wherever the Spirit of the Lord is,[7] and he sees the gospel invested with a greater glory than attended the administration of the law. When Moses' face gave forth rays of light after his face-to-face encounter with God, he had to cover it with a veil to conceal from the Israelites the fact that this reflected glory was one that gradually vanished away;[8] the ministers of "the gospel of the glory of Christ", on the other hand, beholding "the light of the knowledge of the glory of God in the face of Christ", suffer no gradual diminution of that glory reflected in their lives. Instead, they experience an increasing transformation into the likeness of Christ "from one degree of glory to another" through the operation of "the Lord who is the Spirit".[9] Those who hear the "old covenant" read without the illumination imparted by the new covenant which God has now established with His people have their faces covered like Moses' face, covered with a veil which interposes between them and the unfading glory of Christ; but as with Moses, so with them: "when a man turns to the Lord, the veil is taken away."[10]

Of all the New Testament writings it is the Epistle to the Hebrews that chiefly presents the pattern of promise and fulfilment in terms of the two covenants, to the point where it could be designated by Geerhardus Vos "the Epistle of the Diatheke".[11] Perhaps, however, it is going too far to conceive of the contents of this epistle solely, or even mainly, in terms of the covenant principle; a good part of its argument is conducted without express reference to covenant. Yet the contrast between the old covenant and the new makes a substantial contribution to the argument.

---

[1] Cf. Ezek. 36:26.   [2] II Cor. 3:3, 6.   [3] II Cor. 3:14.
[4] Lev. 18:5, quoted in Gal. 3:12; Rom. 7:10; 10:5; Luke 10:28.
[5] Deut. 27:26, quoted in Gal. 3:10.
[6] In II Cor. 3:7 it is called "the dispensation of death".
[7] II Cor. 3:17.
[8] Ex. 34:29-35, expounded in II Cor. 3:12-15.
[9] II Cor. 3:16-4:6.
[10] II Cor. 3:16, quoting Ex. 34:34.
[11] "Hebrews, the Epistle of the Diatheke", *PTR* 13 (1915), pp. 587 ff.; 14 (1916), pp. 1 ff.

forth in the Old Testament characters of Hagar and Sarah: "these women are two covenants: one is from Mount Sinai, bearing children for slavery; she is Hagar", whereas Sarah, by implication, represents the new covenant, enjoyed by citizens of "Jerusalem above", the mother-city of the free.[1] This allegorization of the Old Testament story turned its natural meaning upside down, for the Jews traced their descent from Sarah, while Hagar was the mother of a group of Arab tribes, the Ishmaelites – Gentiles, albeit descended from Abraham. But the allegorization is in line with Paul's insistence that the true offspring of Abraham are those who reproduce Abraham's faith, whether they be Jews or Gentiles.

In the Corinthian correspondence the expression "the new covenant" occurs here and there. The best known occurrence is in I Corinthians 11:25, where our Lord's words of institution are quoted in the form: "This cup is the new covenant in my blood". In the Synoptic Evangelists' accounts of the institution "the new covenant" appears in the longer text of Luke ("This cup which is poured out for you is the new covenant in my blood"),[2] but in Mark's narrative (followed by Matthew) the best attested reading has simply "This is my covenant blood which is poured out for many".[3] But while the adjective "new" is absent from this reading (probably the most primitive extant form, even if I Corinthians antedates the Gospel of Mark by a decade), it is nevertheless implied. It is difficult not to discern in Jesus' words an echo of the words of Moses: "Behold the blood of the covenant which Yahweh has made with you according to all these words"[4] – this allusion is more probable than an allusion to Zechariah 9:11, "because of the blood of my covenant with you, I will set your captives free from the waterless pit."[5] The implication is that the covenant of which Jesus speaks is the covenant foretold by Jeremiah, superseding the covenant of Moses' day.

Whereas the covenant with Abraham is fulfilled in Christ, the covenant of Moses' day is "antiquated"[6] in Christ, to be replaced by a new one. By two New Testament writers in particular the relation between the Mosaic covenant and the new covenant is drawn out in some detail – namely by Paul and the writer to the Hebrews.

Paul in II Corinthians 3 contrasts the writing on tablets of stone (the decalogue, associated with the Mosaic covenant) with the writing on "tablets of human hearts" ("hearts of flesh") – an allusion not only to Jeremiah 31:33, where under the new covenant God promises to write His law on His people's hearts, but also to Ezekiel 11:19 f., where He says, "I will take the stony heart out of their flesh and give them a heart of flesh, that they may walk in my statutes and keep my ordinances and obey

---

[1] Gal. 4:21-31. See p. 18 above.
[2] Luke 22:20, relegated to a footnote in RSV as textually doubtful (see p. 99 below).
[3] Mark 14:24 // Matt. 26:28; Matthew adds the epexegetic phrase "for the remission of sins".
[4] Ex. 24:8.   [5] See p. 102 below.   [6] Heb. 8:13.

share the faith of Abraham, for he is the father of us all."[1] By such faith those who once were "strangers to the covenants of promise" become "members of the household of God".[2]

The writer to the Hebrews deals in the same way with the promise made to Abraham: he explains the terms of God's oath to Abraham in Gen. 22:16 f. as follows:

> Since he had no one greater by whom to swear, he swore by himself, saying, "Surely I will bless you and multiply you". And thus Abraham, having patiently endured, obtained the promise [i.e. the words of promise as distinct from their fulfilment]. Men indeed swear by a greater than themselves, and in all their disputes an oath is final for confirmation. So when God desired to show more convincingly to the heirs of the promise the unchangeable character of his purpose, he communicated it with an oath, so that through two unchangeable things, in which it is impossible that God should prove false [namely His promise and the oath which confirmed it], we who have fled for refuge might have strong encouragement to seize the hope set before us.[3]

This hope is bound up with Christ, who has entered the celestial sanctuary on His people's behalf. Abraham is singled out pre-eminently as the man who received the promises, and the writer leaves his readers in no doubt that Christ is the one in whom these promises find their consummation.[4]

Thus Luke, Paul and the writer to the Hebrews alike see a straight line drawn from Abraham to the gospel: the promise made to Abraham points on to Christ and is fulfilled in Him.

But the covenant with Abraham is not the only covenant of Old Testament history which figures in the New Testament. The law, which according to Paul was incompetent to annul or modify the promise to Abraham, was itself associated with a covenant – the covenant whose constitution was written down by Moses in the book which he read to the Israelites at the foot of Mount Sinai, the covenant which, when they accepted its terms, was ratified by the sacrificial blood thrown partly on the altar, representing Yahweh, and partly on the people.[5] This is the covenant referred to by Yahweh in Jeremiah's "new covenant" oracle as "the covenant which I made with their fathers when I took them by the hand to bring them out of the land of Egypt" – the covenant which is to be replaced by a new one whose terms will be written not in a book or on tablets of stone but in the hearts of the house of Israel.[6]

These two covenants – the Sinai covenant and the new covenant which supersedes it – are viewed by Paul in Galatians 4:24 as allegorically set

---

[1] Rom. 4:13-16.   [2] Eph. 2:12, 19.   [3] Heb. 6:13-18.
[4] Heb. 6:19 f.; cf. 7:6; 11:17. The writer of Hebrews uses the expression "to receive the promises" both of receiving the actual promises (as here) and of receiving their fulfilment (as in 11:39).
[5] Ex. 24:3-8. When this passage is summarized in Heb. 9:19 f., the book replaces the altar as representing Yahweh.
[6] Jer. 31:31-34.

the most archaic units in the New Testament. There is some affinity between them and some of the *Psalms of Solomon* of the mid-first century B.C., with their revived hope of the restoration of the Davidic monarchy.[1] This restoration, foretold by God's "holy prophets from of old", was viewed as being essentially the fulfilment of the covenant with Abraham. This covenant is presented to Luke's readers as realized in the gospel.

The same line is taken in some of the speeches in Luke's second volume. Peter, for example, in the temple in Jerusalem concludes in the following terms a speech which is also commonly accepted as primitive:

> You are the sons of the prophets and of the covenant which God gave to your fathers, saying to Abraham, "In your posterity shall all the families of the earth be blessed." God, having raised up his Servant, sent him to you first, to bless you in turning every one of you from your wickedness.[2]

The covenant with Abraham is fulfilled in God's raising up Jesus and sending Him as Saviour to Abraham's descendants in the first instance.

Paul in his turn speaks to the same effect. God's covenant with Abraham is embodied in the promises which "were made to Abraham and to his offspring": this is the "covenant previously ratified by God" which cannot be annulled or even modified by the law which was promulgated 430 years later.[3] Paul, however, insists that Abraham's offspring to which the inheritance was secured by God's covenant is not exclusively, and not necessarily, his offspring "according to the flesh" but "according to the spirit". Abraham's offspring is primarily Christ – we recall the argument that the Greek word *sperma* is singular, and can therefore refer to an individual as well as to a plurality of descendants – and then the sum-total of those who belong to Christ: "if you are Christ's then you are Abraham's offspring, heirs according to promise."[4] The promise to Abraham, "in you shall all the nations be blessed", is finding its realization in the Gentile mission: "those who are men of faith are blessed with Abraham who had faith."[5]

Having treated the subject along these lines in Galatians, Paul comes back to it in Romans: to Israel belong, among other things, "the covenants... and the promises";[6] nevertheless, "not all who are descended from Israel belong to Israel, and not all are children of Abraham because they are his descendants".[7] It is the children of the promise who are the true heirs of Abraham: "the promise to Abraham and his descendants, that they should inherit the world, did not come through the law but through the righteousness of faith... it depends on faith, in order that the promise may rest on grace and be guaranteed to all his descendants – not only to the adherents of the law [Jews] but also to those [Gentiles included] who

---

[1] See pp. 76 f. below.   [2] Acts 3:25 f.   [3] Gal. 3:16 f.
[4] Gal. 3:16, 21-29.   [5] Gal. 3:8 f.
[6] Rom. 9:4; an early and strongly attested variant reads the singular "covenant" (P^{46} B etc.).
[7] Rom. 9:6 f.

CHAPTER V

THE PEOPLE OF GOD

*"I will be your God,
and you shall be my people."*

1. *The Heirs of the Covenant*

IN THE BENEDICTUS (THE SONG OF ZECHARIAH INCORPORATED IN LUKE'S nativity narrative) the Lord God of Israel is praised because He has remembered "his holy covenant" – namely, "the oath which he swore to our father Abraham, to grant us that we, being delivered from the hand of our enemies, might serve him without fear."[1] The oath is presumably that of Genesis 22:16 ff., where Yahweh swears by Himself that Abraham's descendants will increase in strength and numbers and "possess the gate of their enemies", so that their name will become a byword for blessing among all nations. In the narrative of Genesis 22 this sworn promise is not explicitly called a covenant, but in Zechariah's canticle it is brought into close association with the parallel narrative of Genesis 17, where God (El Shaddai) establishes His covenant with Abraham and undertakes to make him the father of a multitude of nations.

> I will make you exceedingly fruitful; and I will make nations of you, and kings shall come forth from you. . . . And I will give to you, and to your descendants after you, the land of your sojournings, all the land of Canaan, for an everlasting possession; and I will be their God.[2]

The men of New Testament days were not concerned with the documentary analysis of the Pentateuch and did not mentally label Genesis 17 "P" and Genesis 22 "JE"; in any case, according to the prevalent documentary analysis the covenant of Genesis 17 is in large measure the counterpart of the oath of Genesis 22, so that one way or the other the collocation of the two passages in the *Benedictus* is soundly based. The same note is struck by Mary in the *Magnificat*:

> He has helped his servant Israel
>   in remembrance of his mercy,
> as he spoke to our fathers,
>   to Abraham and his posterity for ever.[3]

The canticles in Luke's nativity narrative have been recognized as among

---
[1] Luke 1:72 f.   [2] Gen. 17:6-8.   [3] Luke 1:54 f.

powers.¹ In the teaching of Jesus it finds expression in the parable of the invasion of the strong man's fastness and the plundering of his goods by a stronger than himself.² In the Pauline writings we have the picture of the crucified Christ disarming the hostile "principalities and powers" and driving them in triumph before Him.³

But above all it is in the Apocalypse, that "rebirth of images", as A. M. Farrer has called it, that the primaeval motif of conflict comes into its own again, this time to depict the Christian salvation. The seven-headed dragon, the age-old antagonist of righteousness, is identified with the old serpent of Eden and with the malevolent accuser of God's elect.⁴ But the victory over him and his minions is won in a new fashion. The conqueror-in-chief is the Davidic Messiah, "the lion of the tribe of Judah", who appears, however, as the sacrificed Lamb restored to life after winning his victory by submission to death;⁵ his followers share his victory by similar submission. When the dragon assaults them, calling up Antichrist, portrayed as the beast from the sea, to make war against them, "they have conquered him by the blood of the Lamb and by the word of their testimony, for they loved not their lives even unto death".⁶ This victory is hailed as the final manifestation and vindication of the Saviour God; it is greeted by a loud voice proclaiming in heaven: "Now the salvation and the power and the kingdom of our God and the authority of his Christ have come."⁷ And the seal is set on the victory by one last reference to the unruly deep: when John sees the first heaven and earth pass away to be replaced by a new heaven and a new earth, he adds with emphasis, "and the sea was no more".⁸

---

¹ Mark 4:35–41 followed by Mark 5:1–20 (and parallels). The conflict and victory motif is specially marked in the Matthaean account; cf. G. Bornkamm *et alii*, *Tradition and Interpretation in Matthew*, E. T. (London, 1963), pp. 52 ff.
² Mark 3:27 (and parallels).
³ Col. 2:15.
⁴ Rev. 12:9 (see p. 44, n. 2 above).
⁵ Rev. 5:5 ff.
⁶ Rev. 12:11.
⁷ Rev. 12:10.
⁸ Rev. 21:1.

THE VICTORY OF GOD

> Rejoice greatly, O daughter of Zion!
> Shout aloud, O daughter of Jerusalem!
> Lo, your king comes to you:
> triumphant and victorious is he ... .[1]

"Triumphant and victorious is he" (RSV) might be more literally rendered "righteous and blest with salvation is he" – a description almost identical with that of Yahweh in Isa. 45:21.[2] Zion's king comes in Yahweh's name to accomplish Yahweh's work.

So, in the gospel record, Jesus' entry into Jerusalem in fulfilment of Zech. 9:9 presents him as the king who comes in the name of the Lord to accomplish His victory for the deliverance of His people. In Him, according to the consensus of New Testament witness, the God of Israel has brought His salvation near, revealing Himself, in Paul's words, as "just and the justifier of him who has faith in Jesus".[3] The presentation of the redemptive work of Christ in terms of the Exodus motif in so many strands of New Testament teaching shows how primitive was the Christian use of this motif – going back, quite probably, to the period of Jesus' ministry. Jesus' contemporaries freely identified Him as a second Moses – the expectation of a second Moses played an important part in popular eschatology at the time[4] – and with the expectation of a second Moses went very naturally the expectation of a second Exodus. One might have thought, in view of the identity of name, that Jesus would have been more readily thought of as a second Joshua ("Yahweh is salvation"). The second Joshua concept does indeed appear here and there in the New Testament[5] – and the saving significance of the name is made explicit in Matt. 1:21 ("you shall call his name Jesus, for he will save his people from their sins") – but the second Moses concept is much more prominent. The coincidence of Jesus' death with the Passover season no doubt helped the interpretation of His work as a new Exodus, in which the God of Israel had once more "visited and redeemed his people."[6]

Traces are not lacking, either, even in the New Testament, of the conflict imagery which was repeatedly used in Old Testament times to set forth the saving act of God. It appears in one form in the gospel narratives of the stilling of the tempest on the Sea of Galilee, where Jesus shows Himself the master of wind and wave, as in the story of the legion-possessed Gerasene which follows He shows Himself conqueror of the demonic

---

[1] Zech. 9:9 (see pp. 106 f. below).
[2] Cf. ṣaddîq wᵉ-nôshāʻ huʼ in Zech. 9:9 with ṣaddîq ū-môshîaʻ in Isa. 45:21.
[3] Rom. 3:26.
[4] As the Qumran texts have shown; the Old Testament *testimonium* chiefly quoted being Deut. 18:15 ff. (cf. John 1:21; 6:14; 7:40; Acts 3:22 f.; 7:37); see F. F. Bruce, *Biblical Exegesis in the Qumran Texts* (London, 1960), pp. 46 ff.
[5] Cf. Heb. 4:8 (the leader into the earthly "rest" of Canaan bears the same name as the leader into "the rest that remains for the people of God").
[6] Luke 1:68.

> Yahweh goes forth like a mighty man,
> > like a man of war[1] he stirs up his fury;
> he cries out, he shouts aloud,
> > he shows himself mighty against his foes.[2]

Even the ancient conflict imagery is invoked once again, to link this new deliverance with those which Yahweh wrought in ages past. So Yahweh's power is apostrophized:

> Awake, awake, put on strength,
> > O arm of Yahweh;
> awake, as in days of old,
> > the generations of long ago.
> Was it not thou that didst cut Rahab in pieces,
> > that didst pierce the dragon?
> Was it not thou that didst dry up the sea,
> > the waters of the great deep;
> that didst make the depths of the sea a way
> > for the redeemed to pass over?[3]

This appeal is followed immediately by the assurance:

> And the ransomed of Yahweh shall return
> and come with singing to Zion.[4]

As then, so now; as Yahweh once brought His people out of Egypt, so He will now bring them back from their captivity in Babylonia.

5. *The Final Victory*

It is in Isaiah 40–55 more than anywhere else in the Old Testament that Yahweh's essential character as the God of salvation is emphasized. He is repeatedly called His people's *gō'ēl*, their kinsman-redeemer;[5] He brings near His righteousness[6] which is at once His own victorious vindication and the deliverance of His people; He alone is Yahweh, "and beside me", He says, "there is no saviour":[7]

> a righteous God and a Saviour;
> there is none beside me.[8]

"A righteous God and a Saviour" – practically the same two epithets are given by a later prophet to the future king whom he describes as coming for the salvation of Jerusalem from other overlords than the Babylonians:

---

[1] Heb. *'sh milḥāmāh*, as in Ex. 15:3.   [2] Isa. 42:10–13.
[3] Isa. 51:9 f.   [4] Isa. 51:11; cf. 35:10.
[5] E.g. in Isa. 41:14; 43:14; 44:6, 24; 47:4; 48:17; 49:7, 26; 54:5, 8.
[6] His *ṣᵉdāqāh*, with which the terms for "victory" or "salvation" (*yeshaʻ, yᵉshūʻāh, tᵉshūʻāh*) stand in synonymous parallelism (e.g. in Isa. 46:13); cf. p. 44, n. 5, p. 47, n. 3.
[7] Isa. 43:11.   [8] Isa. 45:21.

> Let the floods clap their hands;
>> let the hills sing for joy together
> before Yahweh, for he comes
>> to rule the earth.
> He will judge the world with righteousness,
>> and the peoples with equity.[1]

4. Return from Exile

A day dawned when the language of the national liturgy seemed to have come true in history on a scale unexampled since the Exodus, when Israel's God, by bringing His people back from the Babylonian captivity, vindicated His reputation as a Saviour God in a manner that gave the lie to all those who assured them mockingly that He was either unable or unwilling to deliver them.

> O sing to Yahweh a new song,
>> for he has done marvellous things!
> His right hand and his holy arm
>> have gotten him victory.
> Yahweh has made known his victory,
>> he has revealed his vindication in the sight of the nations.
> He has remembered his steadfast love and faithfulness to the house of Israel.
> All the ends of the earth have seen
>> the victory of our God.[2]

This celebration of Yahweh's victory – that is, His salvation[3] – finds a clear echo in the context of the return from exile, in the oracles of Isaiah 40–55. In lyric modes drawn from the ancient liturgy[4] the prophet cries:

> Sing to Yahweh a new song,
>> his praise from the end of the earth!
> Let the sea roar and all that fills it,
>> the coastlands and their inhabitants.
> Let the desert and its cities lift up their voice,
>> the villages that Kedar inhabits;
> let the inhabitants of Sela sing for joy,
>> Let them shout from the top of the mountains.
> Let them give glory to Yahweh,
>> and declare his praise in the coastlands.

---

[1] Psalm 98:7-9.
[2] Psalm 98:1-3.
[3] Either word is appropriate as a rendering of Heb. *yesha'* and its cognate forms, according to the context.
[4] Some scholars indeed think that it was the language of Isa. 40–55 that influenced the liturgy and not *vice versa*; cf. N. H. Snaith, according to whom, even if a pre-exilic New Year festival existed in Israel, Psalms 93 and 95–99 "could never have belonged to it, for they are demonstrably dependent upon Second-Isaiah" (The Psalms: *A Short Introduction*, London, 1945, p. 19; cf. also his *The Jewish New Year Festival*, London, 1947, pp. 195 ff.).

But before this – before he comes to recount his personal experience of deliverance – he recalls the doings of Yahweh in the past, with special reference to his mighty works at the Exodus:

> Come and see what God has done:
> > he is terrible in his deeds among men.
> He turned the sea into dry land;
> > men passed through the river on foot.[1]

Yahweh's character, the psalmist implies, is consistent from age to age; the private salvation which he himself has experienced is all of a piece with the national salvation which his people have experienced at Yahweh's hands from the Exodus onwards.

If a private worshipper can express his praise in terms like these, much more can the king of Israel, the embodiment of his people's welfare, do so. In Psalm 18 the royal worshipper celebrates a great deliverance which he himself has experienced, when Yahweh flew to his relief, riding on a cherub, soaring on the wings of the wind, thundering and lightening as he came.

> Then the channels of the sea were seen,
> > and the foundations of the world were laid bare,
> at thy rebuke, O Yahweh,
> > at the blast of the breath of thy nostrils.
> He reached from on high, he took me,
> > he drew me out of many waters.
> He delivered me from my strong enemy,
> > and from those who hated me;
> > for they were too mighty for me.[2]

The theophany here described has elements which recall the creation conflict and others which recall the dividing of the Red Sea and the manifestation of divine power on Mount Sinai. Whether an actual deliverance from foreign foes is being celebrated here (as the general wording of the psalm strongly suggests) or the reference is to the king's ritual combat with the forces of chaos which threatened to overwhelm him and his nation,[3] God's intervention on his behalf is portrayed in language hallowed by ancestral use. Yahweh is the God who "makes great the deliverances of his king and performs covenant-loyalty to his anointed".[4]

As such Yahweh's name is extolled in the national liturgy; His saving victory in the past, reproduced repeatedly in the present, will have its climax on a day yet future:

> Let the sea roar, and all that fills it;
> > the world and those who dwell in it!

---

[1] Psalm 66:5 f.   [2] Psalm 18:15–17.
[3] The latter view is maintained by A. R. Johnson, *Sacral Kingship in Ancient Israel* (Cardiff, 1955), pp. 107 ff.
[4] Psalm 18:50.

> Thou wentest forth for the salvation of thy people,
> > for the salvation of thy anointed.
> Thou didst crush the head of the wicked,
> > laying him bare from thigh to neck. . . .
>
> Thou didst trample the sea with thy horses,
> > the surging of mighty waters.[1]

The memory of Yahweh's past victories, especially at the Exodus, to which the worshippers were very much alive at the Feast of Tabernacles, encourages the prophet to expect His intervention afresh for His people's salvation, whether it be by bringing trouble upon the foreign invaders[2] or by restoring the fertility of the land:

> Though the fig tree do not blossom,
> > nor fruit be on the vines,
> the produce of the olive fail
> > and the fields yield no food,
> the flock be cut off from the fold
> > and there be no herd in the stalls,
> yet I will rejoice in Yahweh,
> > I will joy in the God of my salvation.[3]

The salvation which Yahweh's victory had procured in the beginning was a salvation continually renewed – in the order of nature as in the history of Israel – and ultimately to be consummated on the day of Yahweh. This bringing together of the past, present and future is celebrated at the end of Psalm 29, perhaps another composition for the Tabernacles liturgy:

> Yahweh sits enthroned over the flood;
> > Yahweh sits enthroned as king for ever,
> May Yahweh give strength to his people!
> > May Yahweh bless his people with peace![4]

3. Personal Deliverances

Even in the celebration of personal deliverances the Exodus deliverance is almost bound to be introduced in the Israelite tradition. In Psalm 66, for example, a private worshipper gathers his friends about him as he enters the temple to give thanks to God for some signal deliverance and fulfil the vows which he had undertaken when he was in distress:

> Come and hear, all you who fear God,
> > and I will tell what he has done for me.
> I cried aloud to him,
> > and he was extolled with my tongue.[5]

---

[1] Hab. 3:8–15.   [2] Hab. 3:16.
[3] Hab. 3:17 f., a remarkable expression of joy in God for His own sake, even in the absence of the blessings customarily expected from Him.
[4] Psalm 29:10 f.; cf. A. R. Johnson, *Sacral Kingship in Ancient Israel* (Cardiff, 1955), pp. 54 ff. See also pp. 22 f. above.
[5] Psalm 66:16 f.

> Though thou didst smite Lôtân the fleeing serpent,
> Didst destroy the twisting serpent,
> The accursed one of seven heads.[1]

The Old Testament records establish the many-headed nature of Leviathan, but do not give the exact number of his heads; this the Ugaritic text does, and incidentally supplies a background for the seven-headed dragon of the New Testament Apocalypse and the still later *Odes of Solomon*.[2]

2. The Annual Victory Day

The autumnal equinox, as we have seen, was the occasion for the greatest festival of the agricultural year of Israel, the harvest thanksgiving at which they acknowledged the goodness of Yahweh in providing the fruits of the earth during the preceding season and prayed for a continuation of His mercy throughout the ensuing year. This festival may well have been the setting for the "prayer of Habakkuk the prophet" which appears in our traditional text as an epilogue to his oracle.[3] The oracle is concerned with deliverance from oppression by human enemies, while the prayer is concerned more with deliverance from pestilence, drought and famine; but in either case the deliverance comes from one and the same God, "the God of my salvation", as the prophet calls Him.[4] The potency of the ancient imagery of Yahweh's victory over the unruly sea appears in the prophet's use of it here to celebrate Yahweh's deliverance of His people from natural calamities; this may indeed reflect the part played by this imagery in the liturgy for the Feast of Tabernacles.

> Was thy wrath against the rivers, Yahweh?
> Was thy anger against the rivers,
> or thy indignation against the sea,
> when thou didst ride upon thy horses,
> upon thy chariot of victory? . . .[5]
>
> The mountains saw thee, and writhed;
> the raging waters swept on;
> the deep gave forth its voice,
> it lifted its hands on high. . . .[6]

---

[1] Text 67: 1:1-3. The Ugaritic adjectives qualifying the repeated "serpent" in this extract (*brḥ* and *'qltn*) are the exact equivalents of the Hebrew adjectives so employed in Isa. 27:1 – *bāriaḥ* (as in Job 26:13; see p. 41, n. 8) and *'aqallāṭōn* (not found elsewhere in the Hebrew Bible).

[2] Rev. 12:3 (cf. the seven-headed "beast" of Rev. 13:1; 17:3); Ode of Solomon 22:5.

[3] Hab. 3:1 ff.; cf. J. H. Eaton, *Obadiah, Nahum, Habakkuk and Zephaniah* (Torch Commentaries, London, 1961), pp. 108 ff.; W. F. Albright, "The Psalm of Habakkuk", *Studies in Old Testament Prophecy presented to T. H. Robinson*, ed. H. H. Rowley (Edinburgh, 1950), pp. 1 ff.

[4] Hab. 3:18.

[5] "Victory" is the RSV rendering here of *yᵉshû'āh*, elsewhere rendered "salvation" (see p. 47, n. 3, p. 48, n. 6).

[6] Perhaps the most striking personification of "the deep" (Heb. *tᵉhōm*) in the Bible.

The language shows plainly that it is drawn from the story of the creation conflict, and there are explicit creation motifs in the context; but it is not the creation that is uppermost in the psalmist's mind.

Another psalmist, at a time when the royal house of David has fallen on evil days, calls upon Yahweh to remember not only His covenanted promises to David but also the display of His power at the Exodus, and describes that display of power in terms of the creation conflict:

> O Yahweh, God of hosts,
> who is mighty as thou art, O Yahweh,
> with thy faithfulness round about thee?
> Thou dost rule the raging of the sea;
> when its waves rise, thou stillest them.
> Thou didst crush Rahab like a carcass,
> thou didst scatter thy enemies with thy mighty arm.[1]

Here the old conflict terminology is transferred to Yahweh's contest on His people's behalf against the power of Egypt. Rahab, the ancient name of the chaos monster, now becomes a name for Egypt; and in fact it appears elsewhere in the Old Testament as a poetic synonym for Egypt, quite apart from this kind of context. Thus in Isa. 30:7 Yahweh exposes the hollowness of promises of aid from Egypt:

> For Egypt's help is worthless and empty,
> therefore I have called her
> "Rahab who sits still".

And in a psalm which brings foreign nations within the range of His mercy Yahweh says: "Among those who know me I mention Rahab and Babylon."[2] Similarly Rahab's dragon associate becomes a figure of the Egyptian king, as in Ezek. 29:3 ff., where Pharaoh Hophra, described as "the great dragon that lies in the midst of his streams", is told that, Leviathan as he is, he will be dragged out of his river with a hook[3] and thrown into the wilderness to be devoured by beasts and birds of prey – a close parallel to the fate of Leviathan in Psalm 74:14.

When another prophet speaks of Yahweh's end-time victory and the final deliverance of His people, the same imagery is used: "In that day Yahweh with his hard and great and strong sword will punish Leviathan the fleeing serpent, Leviathan the twisting serpent, and he will slay the dragon that is in the sea."[4] The dragon in the sea is perhaps the power of Egypt, while Leviathan may well be Assyria or Babylon. It is noteworthy, however, that the double description of Leviathan as "the fleeing serpent, . . . the twisting serpent" is paralleled exactly in the Ugaritic text where Môt ("death") tells Baal that he will overcome him

---

[1] Psalm 89:8–10.   [2] Psalm 87:4.   [3] Cf. Job 41:1.
[4] Isa. 27:1. J. Mauchline includes this passage among those in the "Isaiah Apocalypse" (Isa. 24–27) which "may be genuine Isaianic material" (*Isaiah 1–39*, Torch Commentaries, London, 1962, p. 196).

associate Leviathan. The smiting of the chaos monster is closely associated here and elsewhere with the curbing of the unruly sea, whose constant threat to overflow the cultivated land and spread havoc and disorder made it a ready symbol of chaos. In the Ugaritic texts Yam ("Sea") is personified as a rival power to the Canaanite pantheon; when he demands the surrender of Baal, Baal attacks him with two clubs, vanquishes him and succeeds to the severeignty. Baal's victory thus delivers the ordered land from the menace of the sea.[1]

In another passage in Job Yahweh's action against the sea in the course of his creative work is described without mention of the chaos monster:

> Or who shut in the sea with doors,
>   when it burst forth from the womb;
> when I made clouds its garment,
>   and thick darkness its swaddling band,
> and prescribed bounds for it,
>   and set bars and doors,
> and said, "Thus far shall you come, and no farther,
>   and here shall your proud waves be stayed"?[2]

But whether personification is prominent or not, the God who restrains the raging of the sea is "a God of salvation" because His victory over the sea is the salvation of those who inhabit dry land.

Israel's conception of Yahweh as the God of their salvation was mainly dependent, however, not on His activity in creation but on His action on their behalf at the Exodus. The crossing of the Sea of Reeds was their salvation because it was Yahweh's victory – not only over Pharaoh and his chariotry but over all the gods of Egypt He had "triumphed gloriously".[3]

Not only did this victory and salvation become the pattern for all their future experiences of Yahweh's delivering power; the Exodus itself was portrayed time and again in terms of Yahweh's earlier victory against the forces of chaos. The use of these terms to portray the Exodus was made the easier because in the Exodus, as at the creation, Yahweh manifested His mastery over the sea. If He curbed it at the creation, He divided it at the Exodus. Thus one of the later psalmists, praying for national deliverance in a time of great distress, recalls how Yahweh wrought deliverance for His people at the Exodus, but does so in these words:

> Yet God my King is from of old,
>   working salvation in the midst of the earth.
> Thou didst divide the sea by thy might;
>   thou didst break the heads of the dragons on the waters.
> Thou didst crush the heads of Leviathan,
>   thou didst give him as food for the creatures of the wilderness.[4]

---

[1] Ugaritic texts 137; 133; 68.   [2] Job 38:8-11.
[3] Ex. 12:12; 15:1.   [4] Psalm 74:12-14.

"infant hands" strangling the serpent recalls the story of the infant Heracles[1] strangling with his hands the two serpents which Hera sent to kill him in his cradle.[2] But it is not only the familiar mythology of Greece that underlies Wesley's language.

The picture of a deity or hero procuring deliverance by fighting and conquering a serpent or dragon is widespread in the ancient Near East, and farther afield as well. The dragon may be the dragon of chaos or of drought, or (and this is specially marked in Old Testament literature) he may symbolize some historical figure. In the Old Testament it is uniformly Yahweh who destroys the dragon, no matter what malign power may be denoted by the dragon from one place to another. The functions which in the Canaanite pantheon are shared out among a wide variety of deities are for the Israelites concentrated in Yahweh; in the Ugaritic texts Asherah walks on the sea and Baal rides on the clouds, but in the Old Testament it is Yahweh who does both:[3]

> He plants his footsteps in the sea,
> And rides upon the storm.[4]

So too it is Yahweh who curbs the forces of chaos and brings the ordered world into being; it is Yahweh who delivers His people from the threat of drought and famine and gives them "the grain, the wine and the oil";[5] it is Yahweh who goes forth to war against their human enemies and wins salvation for them.

So far as the curbing of the forces of chaos is concerned, it is not to the creation narratives of Genesis that we look for the pictorial representation of this conflict; there is the barest verbal reminiscence of it in Gen. 1:2, "darkness was upon the face of the deep", if the noun $t^eh\bar{o}m$ ("deep") is cognate with Tiamat, the monster destroyed by Marduk in the Babylonian creation myth. But when the creative might of God is described by Job, the ancient conflict imagery comes to clear expression:

> By his power he stilled the sea;
> by his understanding he smote Rahab.
> By his wind the heavens were made fair;
> his hand pierced the fleeing serpent.[6]

"Rahab" is the monster of chaos,[7] and the "fleeing serpent"[8] is her dragon

---

[1] Cf. W. L. Knox, "The 'Divine Hero' Christology in the New Testament", *HTR* 41 (1948), pp. 229 ff.
[2] Pindar, *Nemean Odes* 1.35 ff.; Theocritus, *Idyll* 24.26 ff., etc.
[3] Cf. Job 9:8; Psalm 77:19; Isa. 19:1; Deut. 33:26.
[4] W. Cowper.   [5] Hosea 2:8.   [6] Job 26:12 f.
[7] Cf. Job 9:13, "God will not turn back his anger; beneath him bowed the helpers of Rahab".
[8] Heb. *nāḥāsh bārīaḥ*; here the adjective is translated "crooked" in AV as is *'aqallāṭōn* in Isa. 27:1 (see p. 44, n. 1); hence the "crooked serpent" of Wesley's lines quoted above.

CHAPTER IV

THE VICTORY OF GOD

"I will sing to the Lord, for he has triumphed gloriously."

1. Defeating the Dragon

THE SALVATION OF GOD IS THE VICTORY OF GOD: AS AT THE EXODUS, SO in the redemptive act of Christ the victory of God is the salvation of His people. The Hebrew words for "salvation" are readily translated "victory" in our common English versions when the context makes this rendering preferable.

The Old Testament portrayal of the divine victory is sometimes couched in a form of conflict imagery which survives into New Testament times and even into Christian hymnody, and which reminds us vividly of the environment in which Israel's faith came to birth and grew up. If we follow the course of this conflict imagery we shall be going over the same ground as we have covered in the preceding chapter, but in different terms.

In one of his lesser-known hymns on the nativity, Charles Wesley acclaims the infant Christ in these words:

> Gaze on that helpless Object
> Of endless adoration!
> Those infant hands shall burst our bands
> And work out our salvation;
> Strangle the crooked serpent,
> Destroy his works for ever,
> And open set the heavenly gate
> To every true believer.[1]

We know what Wesley means: he is expressing in poetical language the New Testament teaching that "the reason the Son of God appeared was to destroy the works of the devil";[2] that the purpose of his incarnation was "that through death he might destroy him who has the power of death, that is, the devil, and deliver all those who through fear of death were subject to lifelong bondage".[3] But where does he go for his imagery?

One of his sources, quite plainly, is Greek mythology: the picture of

---

[1] C. Wesley, *Hymns for the Nativity of our Lord*, vi, stanza 5: *The Poetical Works of John and Charles Wesley*, ed. G. Osborn, iv (London, 1869), p. 112.
[2] I John 3:8b.
[3] Heb. 2:14 f.

Luke the theologian and Luke the historian do not stand in such tension one with the other as is often represented: Luke, at any rate, betrays no consciousness of conflict between his theology and his history. His theology *is* his history – interpreted history, it is true, redemptive history in continuity with the history of salvation in the Old Testament, but still history.[1]

[1] Cf. D. P. Fuller, *Easter Faith and History* (London, 1968); H. Flender, *St. Luke: Theologian of Redemptive History*, E. T. (London, 1967).

Behold, you scoffers, and wonder, and perish;
for I do a deed in your days,
a deed you will never believe, if one declares it to you.[1]

In his report of this sermon, Luke reveals his interest in the history of salvation. In the "Century Bible" commentary on the Gospel of Luke, E. E. Ellis expresses agreement with E. Lohse's designation of Luke as "a theologian of redemptive history", although he differs from Hans Conzelmann by refusing to see a sharp cleavage between "the time of Jesus" and "the time of the church"; he sees a twofold, not a threefold, division in Luke's historical perspective – the time of promise ("the law and the prophets") which lasted till John the Baptist, and the time of fulfilment ("the kingdom of God") which was inaugurated by Jesus but went on after His resurrection.[2] Nevertheless, the ministry of Jesus does mark "the mid-point of time":[3] the mighty works of God recorded in the Old Testament have reached their climax in Him, but the redemptive work which He accomplished in His death and resurrection has continuing effects in history. Luke shows little sign of perplexity over the postponement of the *parousia* – an over-rated factor in New Testament thinking, in any case. What Jesus began to do and teach until the day of His exaltation He has continued to do and teach since that day[4] – no longer indeed in bodily presence on earth but by His Spirit in the apostles. The mighty works and wonders and signs which God did by Him in the midst of His people continued to be done in His name by the apostles and their associates,[5] and so He still manifested His presence with them and sealed to men and women through their ministry the benefits of His redemptive act. The consummation will come: God has appointed a day on which He will judge the world in righteousness by the man whom He has ordained for this.[6] Not only has He given a pledge of this by raising Christ from the dead; the presence and power of the Spirit are a token that the last days have arrived, but the duration of the last days does not affect their character as the last days. Meanwhile the kingdom of God advances. If Luke's narrative ends when he has brought Paul to Rome and leaves him "preaching the kingdom of God and teaching the story of the Lord Jesus Christ" at the heart of the empire without let or hindrance,[7] that is because Rome is the planned goal of his narrative, not because the progress of the gospel has reached its terminus.

---

[1] Acts 13:40 f., quoting Hab. 1:5 (cf. the application of Habakkuk's warning, originally spoken with the Chaldaean invasion in view, to the impending invasion of the Kittim, probably the Romans, in 1Qp Hab 1.16 ff.).

[2] E. E. Ellis, *The Gospel of Luke* (London, 1966), pp. 15 f., quoting E. Lohse, "Lukas als Theologe der Heilsgeschichte", *Evangelische Theologie* 14, 1954–5, pp. 254 ff., and H. Conzelmann, *The Theology of St. Luke* (London, 1960), pp. 149 f., 170.

[3] Cf. the German title of H. Conzelmann's book mentioned in the previous note, *Die Mitte der Zeit* (Tübingen, 1954); also O. Cullmann, *Christ and Time* (London, 1951), pp. 121 ff.; *Salvation in History* (London, 1967), pp. 147, 166 ff., *et passim*.

[4] Acts 1:1 f.   [5] Acts 2:22, 43.   [6] Acts 17:31 (cf. 10:42).   [7] Acts 28:30 f.

upon us hard bondage. Then we cried to Yahweh, the God of our fathers, and Yahweh heard our voice, and saw our affliction, our toil and our oppression; and Yahweh brought us out of Egypt with a mighty hand and an outstretched arm, with great terrors and signs and wonders; and he brought us into this place and gave us this land, a land flowing with milk and honey. . . .

This is a relatively short form of confession; in the course of time it was expanded in the national liturgy into the form which we find in Psalms 78, 105 and 106. Psalm 78 is noteworthy not merely for the amplification of the story of the Exodus, the wilderness and the settlement but also because it carries the recital on to the establishment of David and his dynasty on Mount Zion: in this the psalmist sees the climax of God's mighty acts on His people's behalf.[1]

I remember how illuminating I found the passage in G. E. Wright's book *God Who Acts*, published in 1952, where he points out that the earlier part of Paul's synagogue address at Pisidian Antioch covers the same ground as these early confessions, presenting, we might say, the outline of an Old Testament *kerygma* to serve as prolegomena to its New Testament counterpart.[2]

The God of this people Israel chose our fathers and made the people great during their stay in the land of Egypt, and with uplifted arm he led them out of it. And for about forty years he bore with them in the wilderness. And when he had destroyed seven nations in the land of Canaan, he gave them their land as an inheritance . . . And after that he gave them judges until Samuel the prophet. Then they asked for a king; and God gave them Saul the son of Kish. . . . And when he had removed him, he raised up David to be their king . . .[3]

For conciseness this outline is comparable to the "response" of Deut. 26: 5-10; for chronological scope it corresponds to Psalm 78. But whereas the psalm sees the raising up of David as the climax of saving history, Paul's sermon treats it as a stage on the way to the real climax: "Of this man's posterity God has brought to Israel a Saviour, Jesus, as he promised."[4] When Jesus' enemies had fulfilled all that had been "written" concerning Him by putting Him to death, God reversed their action by raising Him from the dead, thus fulfilling to the children the promise He had made to the fathers. Here then is the good news: "through this man forgiveness of sins is proclaimed to you, and by him every believer is justified from everything from which you could not be justified by the law of Moses."[5] And because it is one continuous history of salvation and the same God who is active throughout its course, words of warning spoken through the prophet Habakkuk at an earlier stage of the history are still applicable:

[1] See pp. 68 ff. below.
[2] G. E. Wright, *God Who Acts* (London, 1952), pp. 70, 81.
[3] Acts 13:17-22. [4] Acts 13:23. [5] Acts 13:27-39.

read "the Lord", others "God" and yet others, giving us no name at all, read "he who saved..." (one papyrus exhibits the conflated reading, "God Christ who saved..."). But the principle that the more difficult reading is to be preferred points to "Jesus" as the original, and indeed the variety of other readings can best be explained as substitutions for "Jesus". "Jesus" in this context cannot be understood as the Greek form of Joshua (as in Acts 7:45; Heb. 4:8), for Joshua neither led Israel out of Egypt nor destroyed the unbelievers in the wilderness. It was Moses who led his people out of Egypt, but Moses did so under superior leadership. It was *the Lord* who "brought the people of Israel out of the land of Egypt by their hosts",[1] it was *the Lord* who "went before them",[2] and it was by the decree of *the Lord* that the "evil generation" that came out of Egypt died in the wilderness.[3] While *Yahweh* stands in the Hebrew text, the Greek version used by Jude, as by other New Testament writers, had *Kyrios* in its place, and for Greek-speaking Christians to whom Jesus was the *kyrios* or Lord *par excellence* it was an easy matter to understand *Kyrios* in the Greek Old Testament to refer to Him.[4] If, again, the actions ascribed to Yahweh in the Exodus and wilderness narratives are elsewhere ascribed to His angel – the one of whom He said "my name is in him"[5] – then the interpretation of this special angel in terms of the Son of God before His incarnation presented no difficulty. Early Christian exegesis of the Old Testament provides many examples of this sort of thing, although New Testament examples are scanty (in Stephen's speech it is perhaps implied that Jesus was "the angel" who appeared to Moses "in a flame of fire in a bush", and later on the day of the assembly at Sinai).[6]

2. A Historian of Salvation

When the Israelite worshipper made a solemn confession of his faith before Yahweh, it tended to take the form of a recital of Yahweh's mighty acts. Professor von Rad pointed this out many years ago[7] in relation to the confession of Deut. 26:5-9, where the Israelite settler in Canaan, presenting the first-fruits of his harvest at the sanctuary, is directed to make this response:

> A wandering Aramaean was my father; and he went down into Egypt and sojourned there, few in number; and there he became a nation, great, mighty and populous. And the Egyptians treated us harshly, and afflicted us, and laid

---

[1] Ex. 12:51.   [2] Ex. 13:21.   [3] Num. 14:20 ff.; Deut. 1:34 ff.
[4] Cf. F. F. Bruce, "Jesus is Lord", in *Soli Deo Gloria*, ed. J. McD. Richards (Richmond, Va., 1968), pp. 23 ff.
[5] Ex. 23:20 f.; cf. 14:19; 32:34; 33:2, 14 ff.
[6] Acts 7:30, 38.
[7] G. von Rad, *Das formgeschichtliche Problem des Hexateuchs* (Giessen, 1938), pp. 3 ff.; E. T. in first chapter of *The Problem of the Hexateuch and Other Essays* (Edinburgh, 1966), pp. 1 ff., esp. pp. 3 ff.

use of the Old Testament in the New – "these things happened to them *typikōs* (by way of example), but they were written down for our instruction, upon whom the end of the ages has come."[1] And the writer to the Hebrews, who also emphasizes that the final salvation has been provided by God "at the end of the ages",[2] underlines the lesson taught by Paul: Israel in the wilderness had a promised rest before them, but failed to enter into it because of unbelief; so Christians may miss the rest that remains for the people of God if they in their turn cherish "an evil heart of unbelief, in falling away from the living God."[3]

When Paul reminds the Corinthian Christians that the Israelites in the wilderness had supernatural food and drink, he has in mind not only the bread from heaven and the water from the rock, but the spiritual and eternal reality to which these pointed. For them, as for the people of God today, Christ was the true source of strength and refreshment: "they drank from the supernatural Rock which followed them, and the Rock was Christ".[4] This statement is not to be illustrated by the rabbinical fancy of the rock which rolled through the desert alongside the Israelites, providing them with water from the first year to the fortieth,[5] but by those Old Testament passages, especially the Song of Moses in Deuteronomy 32, where the God of Israel is His people's Rock. When Jeshurun (Israel) waxed fat and kicked,

> then he forsook God who made him,
> and scoffed at the Rock of his salvation.[6]

But when trouble overcame them because of their sins,

> They remembered that God was their Rock,
> the Most High God their redeemer.[7]

This is an example of a further New Testament principle of Old Testament interpretation – what A. T. Hanson has called the "real presence" of Christ in Old Testament history.[8] This is a principle, I must admit, which I am not over-ready to recognize in the New Testament, and I am even less ready to condone its use by modern scholars as a means of christianizing certain areas of the Old Testament narrative. But its occasional presence in the New Testament is difficult to dispute. Paul's statement that "the Rock was Christ" is one such occasion. Another is the remarkable statement in the Epistle of Jude, "that Jesus, who saved a people out of the land of Egypt, afterwards destroyed those who did not believe".[9] True, the name "Jesus" is not read in all forms of the text: in its place some authorities

---

[1] I Cor. 10:5-11. [2] Heb. 9:26. [3] Heb. 3:12 ff.
[4] I Cor. 10:4b.
[5] Cf. Pseudo-Philo, *Biblical Antiquities* 10:7; Tosefta *Sukkah* 3:11 f.
[6] Deut. 32:15. [7] Psalm 78:35.
[8] A. T. Hanson, *Jesus Christ in the Old Testament* (London, 1965), p. 7 *et passim*.
[9] Jude 5.

were redeemed from slavery in Egypt and later from captivity in Babylon so in the fulness of time they were redeemed by the sacrifice of Christ from spiritual bondage under "the elemental spirits of the universe".[1]

In some degree the New Testament sees certain phases of the Exodus pattern recapitulated in the personal experience of Christ. What Yahweh says to Pharaoh about Israel, "Israel is my first-born son",[2] is said again from heaven about Jesus: "This is my beloved Son."[3] As Israel went down to Egypt and was brought up again, so Matthew the Evangelist records the descent of the holy family into Egypt and back, and applies to Jesus "what the Lord had spoken by the prophet, 'Out of Egypt have I called my son'."[4] Jesus' forty days of testing in the wilderness of Judaea form a parallel to Israel's forty years of testing in the wilderness – it is not by chance that Jesus' replies to the tempter are all drawn from that context in Deuteronomy where the theme of testing in the wilderness is emphasized[5] – and both periods of testing come as the sequel to a baptismal experience. And, as we have seen, Jesus' passion is described in the Lukan record of the transfiguration as "his exodus which he was to accomplish at Jerusalem".[6]

But it is in the life of the church that the fullest recapitulation of the Exodus motif appears in the New Testament, and the primitive character of this recapitulation is suggested by its pervading Pauline and non-Pauline epistles alike.

Israel was redeemed from Egypt by the paschal lamb, a lamb "without blemish", as the law prescribed;[7] so, says the First Epistle of Peter, Christians have been "ransomed ... with the precious blood of Christ, like that of a lamb without blemish or spot."[8] "Christ our passover was sacrificed for us", says Paul, and as in Israel the passover sacrifice was followed by the week-long festival of unleavened bread, so "let us ... celebrate the festival ... with the unleavened bread of sincerity and truth"[9] – not for a mere week but for the whole of life. Israel passed through the sea, says Paul again, being thus "baptized unto Moses"; Christians for their part are "baptized into Christ".[10] Israel had manna from heaven and water from the rock to sustain and refresh them in the wilderness; Christians too have their supernatural food and drink.[11] But, despite all these privileges, the generation that came out of Egypt died in the wilderness and never saw the promised land, because of rebellion against God; so Christians should take due warning lest disobedience on their part should bring them into comparable disaster. For – and here we have one of the basic texts for the

---

[1] Rom. 3:24; Gal. 4:3; Col. 4:15, 20.   [2] Ex. 4:22.   [3] Mark 9:7.
[4] Matt. 2:15, quoting Hosea 11:1.
[5] See the quotations from Deut. 8:3; 6:13, 16, in Matt. 4:1-11 // Luke 4:1-13.
[6] Luke 9:31.   [7] Ex. 12:5.   [8] I Pet. 1:19.
[9] I Cor. 5:7 f. The Fourth Evangelist implies that Jesus died on the cross at the hour when the passover lamb was sacrificed, and sees in the omission of the *crurifragium* in His case the antitype to the paschal prescription: "you shall not break a bone of it" (John 19:36, quoting Ex. 12:46).
[10] I Cor. 10:2; Gal. 3:27 (Rom. 6:3).   [11] I Cor. 10:3 f.

Yahweh's bringing Abraham out of Ur and confirming His covenant with him are cited by Ezra in token of His faithfulness and righteousness, together with His subsequent deliverance of the Israelites from Egypt and settling of them in the promised land.[1] So in the New Testament Abraham's faith and obedience are repeatedly held up for the instruction of Christians, and his response to the call of God and departure from his home, "not knowing where he was to go", are invoked by Stephen and the writer to the Hebrews to inculcate the lesson that the people of God, Abraham's spiritual progeny, should always be "strangers and exiles on the earth".[2] "So you see", says Paul, "that it is men of faith who are the sons of Abraham".[3]

After the Exodus narratives themselves, it is in relation to the return from exile in Babylon that the recognizable Exodus vocabulary first reappears. To the exiles comes the oracle through Ezekiel: "As I live, says the Lord Yahweh, surely *with a mighty hand and an outstretched arm*, and with wrath poured out, I will be king over you."[4] So, in Isaiah 40-55, the return is represented in a great variety of ways as a recapitulation of the Exodus from Egypt. Sometimes the recapitulation takes a pictorial form at which we shall look later,[5] but repeatedly language used in the narrative of Exodus is echoed afresh in this new context. If at the Exodus Yahweh saved His people by making "a way in the sea, a path in the mighty waters", so He promises the children of the exile that when they pass through the waters He will be with them: He will make a way in the wilderness and rivers in the desert.[6] As He went before the Exodus generation in a pillar of cloud by day and a pillar of fire by night, a pillar which moved from before them and stood behind them when danger threatened from the rear, so to the later generation the promise is given:

> Yahweh will go before you,
> and the God of Israel will be your rear guard.[7]

And whether it was the wilderness of Sinai or that which lay between Babylon and Judah, of both generations the same words were true:

> They thirsted not when he led them through the deserts;
> he made water flow for them from the rock;
> he cleft the rock and the water gushed out.[8]

Even more detailed are the analogies drawn in the New Testament between the deliverance wrought at the Exodus and "the redemption which is in Christ Jesus". That word "redemption" itself is drawn from the language of the Exodus and the return from exile: as the people of God

---
[1] Neh. 9:7 ff.   [2] Ex. 12:1 ff.; Acts 7:2 ff.; Heb. 11:8 ff.
[3] Gal. 3:7.   [4] Ezek. 20:33.   [5] See pp. 47 f.
[6] Isa. 43:2, 16, 19 (cf. Psalm 77:19).   [7] Isa. 52:12 (cf. Ex. 13:21 f.; 14:19 f.).
[8] Isa. 48:21.

CHAPTER III

THE SALVATION OF GOD

"All flesh shall see the salvation of God."

1. The Exodus Pattern

AT THE EXODUS, WE HAVE SEEN, THE GOD OF ISRAEL WAS PROCLAIMED as everlasting King; equally at the Exodus He was revealed as His people's Saviour. The same Song of the Sea as declares His kingship also declares His saving power:

> Yahweh is my strength and my song,
> and he has become my salvation.[1]

Not surprisingly, therefore, the Exodus provides for the rest of the biblical record a form of language and imagery for communicating the message of salvation.

The Exodus motif, indeed, has been detected in the biblical story before the Exodus from Egypt as well as after it. Thus S. H. Hooke, commenting on the significance of Luke's statement that on the mount of transfiguration Moses and Elijah talked with Jesus about the "exodus" which He was to accomplish at Jerusalem, says:

> We have seen Abraham's Exodus from Ur, the Exodus of Israel under Moses from Egypt, the Exodus of the remnant from Babylon, and the Exodus of the Servant of Yahweh by the way of rejection and death from Israel's dream of national restoration. Now, from the Transfiguration onwards the final Exodus begins. We see Jesus with his face set towards Jerusalem, leading an uncomprehending and reluctant company of followers who were to be the new Israel, carried with him through the waters of death, baptized with his baptism.[2]

In these pregnant sentences the whole biblical outworking of the Exodus motif is compressed. But the Exodus from Egypt determines the main features of the pattern as Abraham's departure from Ur does not. Abraham's departure from Ur is indeed set forth as an example for the people of God in Old and New Testaments alike. "Look to Abraham your father", says the prophet by way of encouragement to the exiles in Babylon, "for when he was but one I called him, and I blessed him and made him many."[3]

---

[1] Ex. 15:2a.
[2] S. H. Hooke, *Alpha and Omega* (London, 1961), p. 181. The Exodus pattern may have influenced the way in which the story of Abraham was told as it influenced the recording of some of the later events mentioned.
[3] Isa. 51:2.

was or was not the King of the Jews – even granted that He was, what significance could a Jewish king or his death have for non-Jews? It is for people like these, living it might be many miles from Jerusalem and several decades after A.D. 30, that the abiding significance of the kingship of Jesus is brought out by John in the form of a conversation between Jesus and Pilate inside the praetorium, where the prosecutors would not follow them lest they should incur ceremonial defilement. Pilate questioned Jesus about His alleged claim to be King of the Jews: Jesus replied that "King" was Pilate's word, not His own, but that His kingship, if that was the term to be used, was not one of which Roman law normally took cognizance. "My kingship is not of this world; if my kingship were of this world, my servants would fight ... For this I was born, and for this I have come into the world, to bear witness to the truth. Every one who is of the truth hears my voice."[1]

Pilate might not be interested, but to many who read these words when first they were published, and to many more who have read them since, they spoke and still speak of a King and a kingdom of enduring importance and authority. The title on the cross might be meant in mockery, but the theme of Christ reigning from the tree is central to Christian belief. The second-century reading of that expression into the text of Psalm 96:10 is a patent corruption,[2] but when the apostles and their colleagues and successors proclaimed among the nations that the Lord was King, the Lord of whom they spoke was the Crucified One. "He must reign", says Paul, "until God has put all his enemies under his feet",[3] but the King who thus reigns at God's right hand is the King who vindicated His sovereignty by the shame and agony of the cross. So, in the Apocalypse, it is as the sacrificed Lamb that He establishes His claim to universal dominion[4] and brings near the day when heaven proclaims: "The kingdom of the world has become the kingdom of our Lord and of his Christ, and he shall reign for ever and ever."[5]

[1] John 18:33-8. Cf. C. H. Dodd, *The Interpretation of the Fourth Gospel* (Cambridge, 1953), pp. 88 f.
[2] Cf. Justin, *Dialogue with Trypho*, 73.
[3] I Cor. 15:25 (echoing Psalm 110:1).
[4] Rev. 5:5-12.
[5] Rev. 11:15.

weh.[1] This would not be the only instance of a reinterpretation of earlier prophecy in the book of Daniel.[2]

It is not so much a matter of direct quotation or of verbal echoes of the Servant Songs (more particularly, of the fourth) among the words of Jesus; it is more the fact that His conception of His life-mission, crowned by suffering and death, is anticipated more clearly in those passages than any others in the Old Testament.

The Servant of Yahweh in the course of his service, accomplishing his Master's pleasure, is not only a prophet, communicating to others with "the tongue of those who are taught" what he himself has heard "morning by morning", and a priest, "sprinkling many nations"; he is a king, "establishing justice in the earth" and imparting his law to the coastlands,[3] a king of the ancient order who 'devotes' his life for his people,[4] entering into suffering and death on their behalf, but emerging victorious on the other side to "divide the spoil with the strong".[5]

3. *So you are a king?*

When Jesus was crucified, the terms of His indictment were published on a placard above His head: "The King of the Jews".[6] So far as the Roman record went, this indicated concisely the reason for His execution. All four Evangelists mention it, so presumably they attached some importance to it; but three of them add no comment. John does add something, but that is only to relate the natural protest of the Jewish authorities at what was an insult (no doubt deliberately calculated) to their people, and the dusty answer they received from Pilate.[7] But in another context John says something else which is very much to the point.

The death of Jesus plays a determinant part in the New Testament, and the New Testament writers see the Old Testament also pointing forward to it. Yet the fact that He was executed as (in some sense) the King of the Jews is not one of the more prominent features of their presentation and interpretation of His death. To synagogue congregations, no doubt, the proclamation that the Messiah had come and suffered in accordance with prophetic scripture was a matter of surprised interest and often also of heated debate. But as the gospel spread more and more widely among the Gentiles, it could not be a matter of great moment to them whether Jesus

[1] Cf. M. Black, "Servant of the Lord and Son of Man", *SJT* 6 (1953), pp. 1 ff.
[2] Cf. the reinterpretation of Balaam's "ships from Kittim" (Num. 24:24) in Dan. 11:30 (where they are applied to Roman vessels off Alexandria in 168 B.C.), and the reapplication to Seleucid invasions (Dan. 11:10, 40) of Isaiah's comparison of the Assyrian invasion to an overflowing flood (Isa. 8:8; cf. p. 66 below).
[3] Isa. 50:4; 52:15a; 42:4.
[4] Like Codrus, the (legendary) last king of Athens (cf. Lycurgus, *Against Leocrates*, 84–87), or the Roman consul P. Decius Mus (Livy, *Hist.* vii. 34 f.).
[5] The subject-matter of this paragraph is expanded in pp. 83–90.
[6] Mark 15:26.   [7] John 19:19–22.

account): "from now on the Son of Man shall be seated at the right hand of the Power of God".[1] The impending suffering of the Son of Man would launch the new age in which he would be vindicated by God and visit men as Saviour and Judge. Or, as the Fourth Gospel puts it, the hour had come for the Son of Man to be glorified: "when you have lifted up the Son of Man, then you will know that I am he."[2]

By His passion Jesus fulfils what was written concerning the Son of Man and unfolds the mystery of the kingdom of God. The hallowing of God's name and the doing of His will are synonymous with the manifestation of His kingdom;[3] and never was His name so truly sanctified as in Him who accepted the cross with the words, "Not my will, but thine, be done".[4] Jesus, in Origen's great word, is revealed as the *autobasileia*.[5]

Nor is this all that can be said. It is repeatedly emphasized that *it is written* that the Son of man must suffer. "The Son of Man goes as it is written of him", said Jesus at the Last Supper,[6] and a few hours later He submitted to the soldiers and police who came to arrest Him with the words, "Let the scriptures be fulfilled."[7] There seems to be no convincing argument for excluding this insistence from His authentic sayings. But if that is so, we may well ask, as He asked His disciples, "How is it written of the Son of Man, that he should suffer many things and be treated with contempt?"[8]

It is not so written in the book of Daniel, even if it is implied there (as it probably is).[9] Nor will the teaching about the atoning efficacy of the suffering of the righteous in the Maccabaean martyrologies[10] satisfy the Gospel references: the books of Maccabees were not "scripture" in the New Testament sense of the term. Although it is unfashionable nowadays to hold that Jesus understood His mission in terms of the Isaianic Servant Songs, I see no more probable explanation of the statements that the Son of Man's sufferings were "written" than that Jesus did just this, and identified the Servant of Yahweh with Daniel's "one like a son of man".[11] It may be that others in Israel made this identification (the Qumran community, for example), and that different individuals or groups should independently identify the two figures is the less surprising if from the first the "one like a son of man" was a re-presentation of the Servant of Yah-

---

[1] Luke 22:69 (cf. Mark 14:62 // Matt. 26:64); the language is drawn from the enthronement-oracle of Psalm 110:1. See pp. 80 f. below.
[2] John 12:23, 32; 8:28.   [3] Matt. 6:9 f. // Luke 11:2.   [4] Mark 14:36.
[5] Origen, *Commentary on Matthew*, 14.7 (on Matt 18:23).
[6] Mark 14:21.
[7] Mark 14:49b. See p. 98 below.
[8] Mark 9:12 (see p. 28, n. 8).
[9] Cf. M. D. Hooker, *The Son of Man in Mark* (London, 1967), pp. 27 ff.
[10] Cf. 2 Macc. 7:37 f.; 4 Macc. 6:28 f.; 17:22 (see p. 99 below).
[11] See pp. 97 ff.

recently by Philipp Vielhauer[1] – that, since the terms "kingdom of God" and "Son of Man" do not occur together in Jesus' teaching, one or the other of them is not original to His teaching, and that, since His proclamation of the kingdom of God is too immovably embedded in the gospel tradition, we must conclude that He did not speak of the Son of Man. Others, less radically, admit to His authentic teaching one class of saying about the Son of Man – either his coming glory[2] or (more rarely) his present humiliation[3] – while questioning whether He anticipated the Evangelists in identifying the Son of Man with Himself.[4]

The fact that, with the exception of Stephen's use of the designation "Son of Man" (the crowd's use of it in John 12:34 is not a real exception), it is found in the New Testament only on the lips of Jesus is a strong argument for His use of it – indeed, for His distinctive use of it. The one exception is instructive, for it is related to one of Jesus' most significant utterances about the Son of Man: "every one who acknowledges me before men, the Son of Man also will acknowledge before the angels of God".[5] When Stephen sees "the heavens opened, and the Son of Man standing at the right hand of God", he has just acknowledged Jesus before the Sanhedrin; now he in turn is acknowledged by the Son of Man, standing at God's right hand as advocate on Stephen's behalf.[6]

Again, because of the close relation of the Son of Man with the kingdom of God, it was unnecessary to mention both together: the one implied the other. Moreover, in the teaching of Jesus as the Evangelists record it, there are two phases in the presentation of each of the two concepts – a present phase marked by restriction and humiliation, and a future phase marked by power and glory. The kingdom of God is present in Jesus' ministry, but it is at the moment beset by limitations; one day soon it will "come with power", the limitations removed.[7] The Son of Man will be glorified, he will be seen as he truly is; "but first he must suffer many things and be rejected by this generation".[8] It is, we gather, the suffering of the Son of Man, otherwise expressed as Jesus' undergoing the baptism of death,[9] that unleashes the full power of the kingdom of God and therewith reveals the glory of the Son of Man. As Jesus was about to enter upon His passion, He assured the chief priests and scribes (according to Luke's

---

[1] P. Vielhauer, "Gottesreich und Menschensohn in der Verkündigung Jesu", in *Festschrift für Günther Dehn* (Neukirchen, 1957), pp. 51 ff.

[2] Cf. A. J. B. Higgins, *Jesus and the Son of Man* (London, 1964), pp. 185 ff. *et passim*; H. E. Tödt, *The Son of Man in the Synoptic Tradition*, E. T. (London, 1965), pp. 32 ff. *et passim*.

[3] Cf. E. Schweizer, *Lordship and Discipleship* (London, 1960), pp. 32 ff.; "The Son of Man Again", *NTS* 9 (1962–63), pp. 256 ff.

[4] Cf. R. H. Fuller, *The Foundations of New Testament Christology* (London, 1965), pp. 119 ff. For a less sceptical assessment see M. D. Hooker, *The Son of Man in Mark* (London, 1967), pp. 77 ff.

[5] Luke 12:8; cf. Mark 8:38.   [6] Acts 7:55.   [7] Mark 9:1.

[8] Luke 17:25. The expression "suffer many things" (cf. Mark 8:31; 9:12) goes back to a primitive stage of the gospel tradition. See p. 98, n. 4.

[9] Luke 12:50 (cf. Mark 10:38 f.).

especially in the *Similitudes of Enoch* – is an interesting study.[1] If it is not pursued here, that is because of the unlikelihood that Jesus' thought was influenced by the *Similitudes of Enoch*, even if the language of some of the Evangelists is influenced by the language of the *Similitudes*.[2] It is in Daniel, not in Enoch, that the main literary source of Jesus' terminology must be sought, although He develops the concepts of Daniel in His own way. There were others in His day who no doubt thought of themselves as belonging to the saints of the Most High, like those ḥăsīḏīm of Psalm 149, with "the high praises of God in their throats and two-edged swords in their hands", who engage in battle against the nations "to bind their kings with chains and their nobles with fetters of iron".[3] And during the Christian era some who claimed to be disciples of Jesus have cast themselves in this rôle, like the "fifth-monarchy" zealot[4] into whose mouth Macaulay's *Battle of Naseby* puts similar language:

> O, evil was the root, and bitter was the fruit,
> And crimson was the juice of the vintage that we trod;
> For we trampled on the throng of the haughty and the strong,
> Who sate in the high places, and slew the saints of God.

How different the way of Jesus was from this interpretation of the rôle of the saints is plain to read in the Gospels. So different was it, in fact, from what was generally expected that even John the Baptist, hearing in prison reports of Jesus' ministry, doubted if this was after all the Coming One whom he had announced, who was to bring the winnowing-fan of judgement to the threshing-floor of Israel and gather the wheat into his barn but burn up the chaff with unquenchable fire.[5] He had to be reassured that in Jesus' ministry the mighty works of the new age were indeed being displayed, as the prophets had foretold, and – most important of all – the poor were having the good news proclaimed to them.[6]

In the Gospel records of Jesus' teaching, the designation "the Son of man" appears repeatedly. It is, I think, certain that at least in its most distinctive occurrences in His teaching the designation means "the one like a son of man" of whom the book of Daniel speaks – the one to whom the everlasting kingdom is given. That the proclaimer of the kingdom of God should speak of the Son of Man in this way is natural. It has been argued, however – twenty-five years ago by H. B. Sharman[7] and more

---

[1] The *Similitudes of Enoch* (I Enoch 37–71), constitute a unit of the Enoch literature of the closing generations B.C. (collected in I Enoch) and one which has not been identified among the Qumran texts (cf. pp. 91 f.). See the discussion by M. D. Hooker, *The Son of Man in Mark* (London, 1967), pp. 33 ff.
[2] Compare Matt. 25:31 with I Enoch 62:5.
[3] Psalm 149:6–8.
[4] Called by Macaulay "Obadiah Bind-their-kings-in-chains-and-their-nobles-with-links-of-iron".
[5] Matt. 3:12 // Luke 3:17.
[6] Matt. 11:2–6 // Luke 7:18–23.
[7] H. B. Sharman, *Son of Man and Kingdom of God* (New York, 1943).

2. The Dominion of the Son of Man

But the proclamation, "The kingdom of God has drawn near", more closely echoed an Old Testament book in which the kingship of God is not expressly associated with David's line. It harks back to the statement in Daniel 7:22 that the appointed time came for the saints to receive the kingdom – the everlasting kingdom which, according to the vision of judgement described and explained in that chapter of Daniel, the God of heaven would establish on the ruins of the pagan world-empires portrayed under the guise of wild beasts. (The same essential pattern appears in Nebuchadnezzar's dream-image composed of four metals, pulverized by the stone cut out without hands, which then becomes a great mountain and fills the whole earth.)[1]

In Daniel's vision this eternal kingdom is bestowed by God, depicted as the Ancient of Days, on "one like a son of man" who comes to Him on the clouds of heaven to receive it.[2] In the angelic interpretation of the vision it is bestowed on "the people of the saints of the Most High".[3] The "one like a son of man" in the vision may be as completely symbolical as the four wild beasts which precede him: as they represent pagan empires so he represents the kingdom of the saints. But the "one like a son of man" – who in any case suggests the humanity of the new kingdom by contrast with the ferocity of the previous ones – has a background which suggests that his status is more ontological: not only is there the kind of background drawn for us by S. Mowinckel[4] and more recently by F. H. Borsch,[5] but there is Adam ("Man") himself, endowed by his Creator with dominion over the earth and all that it contains, in land, sea and air.[6] When the writer to the Hebrews quotes the eighth psalm in which the Genesis account of man's creation is repeated in poetical form, and applies its language to Christ as the Second Man, he may not deliberately bring the "son of man" whom God crowns with glory and honour into association with Daniel's "one like a son of man" but his thought is at least moving on parallel lines to Daniel's.[7] If it is to the "people of the saints of the Most High" that the kingdom is given, it is natural to think of them as having a leader, and no leader is mentioned unless it be the "one like a son of man"; while conversely, if we think of the "one like a son of man" as a figure in his own right, it is natural to provide him with a community of followers. At any rate, in the after-history of Daniel's vision and its interpretation, the individual "son of man" and the "saints of the Most High" appear side by side in close association the one with the other.

The development of the companion concepts of the kingdom of God and the Son of Man in the interval between Daniel and the Gospels –

[1] Dan. 2:31 ff.; see Luke 20:18b for a New Testament interpretation of the stone (cf. p. 66).
[2] Dan. 7:13 f.   [3] Dan. 7:18, 22, 27.
[4] S. Mowinckel, *He That Cometh*, E. T. (Oxford, 1956), pp. 346 ff.
[5] F. H. Borsch, *The Son of Man in Myth and History* (London, 1967), pp. 89 ff.
[6] Gen. 1:26 ff.; Psalm 8:4 ff.   [7] Heb. 2:5 ff.

THE RULE OF GOD

> Sing praises to God, sing praises!
>   Sing praises to our King, sing praises!
> For God is the king of all the earth;
>   sing praises with a psalm!
> God reigns over the nations;
>   God sits on his holy throne.
> The princes of the peoples gather
>   as the people of the God of Abraham.
> For the shields of the earth belong to God;
>   he is highly exalted![1]

While this day lay in the future, there was one area in which Yahweh's kingship was specially manifested and accepted: that was the nation of Israel. So firmly did the conviction of Yahweh's kingship take possession of some groups in Israel that it was felt to be exclusive: since Yahweh was Israel's king, Israel could have no other king. This emerges in Gideon's reply to his grateful fellow-citizens who wished to make him the founder of a hereditary monarchy[2] – even if his words were really a polite acceptance of their offer under the guise of a deprecation of it – and later in Samuel's reaction to the people's demand that he should choose a king for them.[3]

When, however, the monarchy was established, the king was recognized as Yahweh's anointed vicegerent, acceptable in so far as he represented Yahweh's kingship among his people.

> When one rules justly over men,
>   ruling in the fear of God,
> he dawns on them like the morning light,
>   like the sun shining forth upon a cloudless morning,
>   like rain that makes grass to sprout from the earth.[4]

The king was bound to maintain justice and covenant loyalty,[5] and when he failed to do this, he forfeited his right to be king. Yet, with the decline and fall of the Hebrew monarchies, the hope of an ideal vicegerent of Yahweh was not lost: a king would reign in righteousness with princes decreeing justice; then the fruit of righteousness would be peace and the result of righteousness quietness and security for ever.[6] This hope, specially associated with a coming ruler of the house of David, lived on beyond the exile into the Christian era, as we shall see later.

---

[1] Psalm 47:5 ff.; cf. Charles Wesley's christianized version in his hymn "God is gone up on high": he comes quickly in the second stanza to its evangelical interpretation:
> God in the flesh below,
>   For us He reigns above:
> Let all the nations know
>   Our Jesus' conquering love! . . .

[2] Judges 8:22 f.
[3] I Sam. 8:4 f.; 12:12 ff.
[4] II Sam. 23:3b-4.
[5] Cf. the "coronation oath" of Psalm 101: "I will sing of loyalty and of justice . . ."
[6] Isa. 32:1, 17; see also pp. 72 f. below.

> Let the nations be glad and sing for joy,
>> for thou dost judge the peoples with equity
>> and guide the nations upon earth.[1]

At the feast of Booths, therefore, the worshippers celebrated Yahweh's kingship not only as manifested in the past and experienced in the present but also as destined to be revealed on a world-wide scale on a day to come – the day of Yahweh. It may well have been at this yearly celebration that Amos visited Bethel, to assure the worshippers there that the day to which they looked forward so eagerly would be a day of darkness, not of light – a day when Yahweh would punish unrighteousness wherever it was found, and first and foremost in His people Israel.[2] The hymn in praise of Yahweh's creative power, of which three strophes are interspersed among the oracles and visions of Amos, and which was perhaps sung at this festival, should serve them as a reminder of the righteousness and majesty of the God with whom they had to do:

> Lo, he who forms the mountains and creates the wind,
>> and declares to man what is his thought;
> who makes the morning darkness,
>> and treads on the heights of the earth -
> Yahweh, the God of hosts, is his name!

> He who made the Pleiades and Orion,
>> and turns deep darkness into the morning,
>> and darkens the day into night,
> who calls for the waters of the sea,
>> and pours them out upon the surface of the earth,
> Yahweh is his name.

> He who touches the earth and it melts,
>> and all who dwell in it mourn,
> and all of it rises like the Nile,
>> and sinks again, like the Nile of Egypt;
> who builds his upper chambers in the heavens,
>> and founds his vault upon the earth; ...
> Yahweh is his name.[3]

Yahweh's mighty acts in creation and history alike prefigured that coming day when He would be obeyed as King over all the earth. As the worshippers celebrated His acts of the past, so they celebrated His universal sovereignty in words which have provided Christians with a proper psalm for Ascension Day:

> God has gone up with a shout,
>> Yahweh with the sound of a trumpet.

[1] Psalm 67:4.
[2] Amos 5:18 ff.; 3:2.
[3] Amos 4:13; 5:8 f.; 8:5 f.

> The Lord is King, be the people never so impatient:
> he sitteth between the cherubims, be the earth never so unquiet.[1]

The Exodus from Egypt was the great manifestation of this victory in history: it was then that Yahweh "triumphed gloriously" on His people's behalf over the power of Egypt and over the Sea of Reeds. Not only were the horse and his rider thrown into the sea, but the sea itself was curbed and compelled to recede by Him who in the beginning held it in check with His "Thus far and no farther".

> At the blast of thy nostrils the waters piled up,
> the floods stood up in a heap;
> the deeps congealed in the heart of the sea.

So says the "Song of the Sea" which celebrates this victory, and it ends with the proclamation:

> Yahweh will reign for ever and ever.[2]

This historical re-enactment of the primaeval victory was not itself re-enacted, but regularly related and celebrated, in the national worship – notably in the feast of Passover, the significance of which was historicized so that it became a commemoration of this mighty work of Yahweh in place of the pastoral occasion that it originally was.[3]

But notable as the Passover was in Israel's sacred year, there was a festival still more closely associated with the proclamation of Yahweh's kingship – the autumnal harvest-home, "the feast of ingathering at the turn of the year", commonly called the feast of Booths or Tabernacles.[4]

> The earth has yielded its increase;
> God, our God, has blessed us.
> God has blessed us;
> let all the ends of the earth fear him![5]

The God of Israel was also the God of heaven and earth, who bestowed the blessings of harvest on all the nations without discrimination. Therefore the psalm just quoted has the refrain:

> Let the peoples praise thee, O God:
> let all the peoples praise thee![6]

When the peoples did indeed praise the true Fount of every blessing, then Yahweh's royal dominion would be acknowledged universally:

---

[1] Psalm 99:1 ("Great Bible" rendering).
[2] Ex. 15:1, 8, 18. See pp. 33, 42 f. below.
[3] Deut. 16:1.
[4] Ex. 23:16; 34: 22; Deut. 16:13 ff. See pp. 44 f. below.
[5] Psalm 67:6 f.
[6] Psalm 67:3, 5.

CHAPTER II

THE RULE OF GOD

*"The Lord has established his throne in the heavens,
and his kingdom rules over all."*

1. The Rule of God in Early Israel

WHEN JESUS, ACCORDING TO MARK'S NARRATIVE, LAUNCHED HIS Galilaean ministry with the announcement, "The appointed time has fully come and the kingdom of God has drawn near; repent, and believe in the good news",[1] He used language which must have rung a loud bell, or several loud bells, in the minds of those hearers who had some consciousness of their people's heritage.

The kingship of Yahweh, the God of Israel, had been for centuries a dominant theme in the national worship. His sovereignty was manifested at creation in the curbing of the unruly deep:

> Mightier than the thunder of many waters,
>   mightier than the waves of the sea,
>   Yahweh on high is mighty![2]

The re-enactment of this victory over chaos in the annual cult is a question which has been canvassed with animation:[3] to this debate I have no contribution to make. To its re-enactment in the national history, however, we have ample testimony: the chaotic powers of the deep are seen to reassert themselves repeatedly when

> The kings of the earth set themselves,
>   and the rulers take counsel together,
>   against Yahweh and his anointed, saying,
> "Let us burst their bonds asunder,
>   and cast their cords from us."[4]

But the nations' furious raging causes no disturbance on high: Yahweh has set the king of Israel, acclaimed as His son, on Zion, His holy hill, and His decree cannot be thwarted, His kingship is unshakable. In the language of Coverdale's version of 1539, sung to this day in the Anglican Prayer Book version:

---

[1] Mark 1:15.
[2] Psalm 93:4.
[3] Cf. A. R. Johnson, *Sacral Kingship in Ancient Israel* (Cardiff, 1955), pp. 46 ff.
[4] Psalm 2:2 ff.

revelation and response, are fulfilled in Jesus. "We have found him",[1] say the Evangelists and apostolic writers, echoing Philip; this is He. This note of fulfilment is struck throughout, yet not so much one note as a harmony of notes. In Jesus the promise is confirmed, the covenant is renewed, the prophecies are fulfilled, the law is vindicated, salvation is brought near, sacred history has reached its climax, the perfect sacrifice has been offered and accepted, the great priest over the household of God has taken his seat at God's right hand, the Prophet like Moses has been raised up, the Son of David reigns, the kingdom of God has been inaugurated, the Son of Man has received dominion from the Ancient of Days, the Servant of the Lord, having been smitten to death for his people's transgression and borne the sin of many, has accomplished the divine purpose, has seen light after the travail of his soul and is now exalted and extolled and made very high.

The purpose of these lectures, then, is to take a few of the chief themes, motifs or images which are used as vehicles of revelation in the Old Testament and consider how the New Testament writers continue to use them to set forth the perfected revelation in Christ. We shall consider them especially as they relate to the rule of God, the salvation of God, the people of God, and the servant of God.

I do not forget that one of the greatest New Testament scholars of the present century, Rudolf Bultmann, has ruled out the possibility of doing any such thing as has just been proposed. After reviewing the rule of God, the people of God, and the covenant principle in the Old Testament, he concludes that there is in each a built-in contradiction which prevents its realization in history. In New Testament Christianity, he maintains, these ideas are supramundane and eschatological (eschatological in the Bultmannian sense) and there can be no continuity between New Testament Christians and the Old Testament picture of Israel as "an empirical historical entity", living under God's rule in terms of a covenant inaugurated by a historical event.[2] This is bound up with Professor Bultmann's refusal of the "history of salvation" concept as relevant to Christianity rightly so called. By contrast with Israel, he holds, "*the new people of God* has no real history, for it is the community of the end-time, an eschatological phenomenon."[3]

This is not how I read the New Testament. As I read it, it not merely presupposes but positively and repeatedly emphasizes the continuity which Professor Bultmann cannot admit, a continuity which is expressed preeminently in the history of salvation.[4]

---

[1] John 1:45.
[2] R. Bultmann, "Prophecy and Fulfillment" in *Essays on Old Testament Interpretation*, ed. C. Westermann (E. T., London, 1963), pp. 50 ff., esp. p. 71.
[3] R. Bultmann, *History and Eschatology* (Edinburgh, 1957), p. 36.
[4] Cf. O. Cullmann, *Heil als Geschichte* (Tübingen, 1965); E. T., *Salvation in History* (London, 1967); see also pp. 36 ff. below.

forth on any such mission, the success of that mission is assured.¹ All the forms in which the Word acted in Old Testament times are summed up and transcended when the Word now appears in true and full humanity.

As the God of Israel in earlier days dwelt among His people – "let them make me a sanctuary", He said to Moses when He directed him to have the tabernacle constructed, "that I may dwell (Heb. *shākan*) in their midst"² – so now in a more direct and intimate way the dwelling of God is with men, for "the Word became flesh and dwelt (pitched his tabernacle³) among us".

When the tabernacle in the wilderness was completed, "the cloud covered the tent of meeting, and the glory of Yahweh filled the tabernacle".⁴ That was the glory of His abiding presence with His people – His *sh^ekīnāh*, to use the language of post-biblical Judaism. Now that His abiding presence has been manifested in the Word made flesh, says the Evangelist, "we have beheld his glory". In Old Testament days the full radiance of the divine glory was beyond the power of mortal man to contemplate; Moses, by way of a special privilege, was permitted to see its afterglow.⁵ No such limitation is suggested when the glory is unveiled in the incarnate Word.⁶ Moses' request, "I pray thee, show me thy glory", received the response: "I will make all my goodness pass before you, and I will proclaim before you my name Yahweh".⁷ The proclamation or exposition of the ineffable name took the form: "Yahweh, Yahweh, a God merciful and gracious, slow to anger, and abounding in steadfast love and faithfulness..."⁸ – or, in the place of the RSV rendering of this last phrase, we might say "full of grace and truth". And when John tells us of the glory which he and his companions saw in the incarnate Word, he says that it was "full of grace and truth"⁹ – the grace and truth which came through Jesus Christ. The proclamation or exposition of the divine name which Moses heard is now caught up and surpassed in the new revelation: "No one has ever seen God; the only Son, who is in the bosom of the Father, he has made him known."¹⁰

No one image or pattern, no one of the motifs or themes which have been reviewed is adequate in itself for the New Testament presentation of the theology of the Old. Covenant is here, and so pre-eminently is the history of salvation, but what is emphasized throughout the New Testament is that these and other themes, and all the images and motifs of

---

¹ Isa. 40:8; 55:10 f.   ² Ex. 25:8.
³ Gk. ἐσκήνωσεν, akin to σκηνή, "tent", "tabernacle".
⁴ Ex. 40:34; cf. I Kings 8:10 f.; Ezek. 44:4.
⁵ Ex. 33:20–23.
⁶ Cf. also the contrast painted in II Cor. 3:7–4:6 between the fading glory that attended the old covenant and "the glory of God in the face of Christ".
⁷ Ex. 33:18 f.   ⁸ Ex. 34:6.
⁹ Despite the RSV arrangement, the adjective "full" (indeclinable πλήρης) in John 1:14 probably qualifies "glory".
¹⁰ John 1:18; the verb here rendered "make known" is ἐξηγέομαι, so that Jesus might be described as the living "exegesis" of God.

These images are of a terrific potency and they are of the very essence of Israel's religion. Revelation has clothed itself in them and to seek to get rid of them, to demythologize the Old Testament, would be to refuse to make use of the very means by which we may hope to apprehend the ultimate reality. ... They are the images whereby we are enabled to apprehend a reality which consists of a succession of divine events, or better of a continuing divine purpose manifesting itself in events, leading up, as Christians believe, to the supreme event of the Incarnation, when the Word became flesh and accomplished the salvation of mankind.[1]

No one, to my knowledge, has done more helpful or stimulating work in the discerning and drawing out of such images throughout the Old and New Testaments than the late S. H. Hooke. Known in his prime as the pioneer of the "myth and ritual" interpretation of ancient Near Eastern religion, Professor Hooke in his later years returned to his first love, the study and exposition of the Bible, and as Speaker's Lecturer at Oxford from 1956 to 1961 expounded the pattern of the biblical revelation in the studies which were later published under the title *Alpha and Omega*. In such an event as the Exodus, for example, he distinguishes three levels – the level of history, the level of interpretation and "the level of the divine activity itself, transcending and embracing in its eternal reality both the other levels". This third level can be attained only in the light of the climactic revelation in Christ, "illuminating the past, and shining through the images". The controlling principle which governs the selection of images is that they arise "in the recorded encounter between God and man where a response of faith and surrender to the divine purpose takes place".[2] It is the establishment and maintenance of this controlling principle that exercises the necessary check on typological fancy. Thus the pattern is traced throughout both Testaments, ending with the exposition of the divine glory disclosed in Christ. When, with His passion and triumph, all the images had met in the central point of revelation, the gift of the Spirit "made it possible for the Church to begin the exploration and exposition of the glory of the Word Incarnate, thus bringing to completion the total pattern of revelation."[3]

The *locus classicus* of the incarnation of the Word in John 1:14 provides a signal example of the meeting of the earlier images of divine revelation at this critical point. The Word which "became flesh" is (if we confine ourselves to its Hebraic antecedents) that agent of the Almighty by which He created the universe,[4] made Himself known to mankind,[5] declared His purpose[6] and acted for His people's deliverance.[7] When the Word goes

---

[1] N. W. Porteous, *Living the Mystery* (Oxford, 1968), p. 27. See also pp. 93–111 of this work for a study of "Jerusalem–Zion: The Growth of a Symbol".
[2] S. H. Hooke, *Alpha and Omega* (London, 1961), pp. 3 f.
[3] *Op. cit.*, p. 291. [4] Cf. Gen. 1:3 ff.; Ps. 33:6, 9. [5] Cf. Deut. 30:14.
[6] Cf. the recurring clause in prophetic literature: "the word of Yahweh came to me"
[7] Cf. Ps. 107:20.

Testament witness to God: "election and covenant, rejection and restoration, *Heilsgeschichte*, creation, and providence, the way of life and the way of death".[1] He went on to say that "if all the copies of the Old Testament were lost or destroyed, any scholar who could remember the text of the Psalms would have at his disposal the essential materials for an Old Testament theology; for the Psalter is, in a sense, the first of all Old Testament theologies"[2] – not systematized, but singable. And when we pass from the Old Testament and consider the decisive part played by the Psalter in the "sub-structure" of *New* Testament theology, its importance for the whole range of biblical theology is underlined.

It is possible to treat the New Testament to some degree in the way in which Professor Anderson has treated the Psalter, not indeed as a creed to be sung rather than signed but as a fresh presentation and interpretation of Old Testament theology – fresh, in the light of the "new thing" that God did in the earth when His Son became man for man's salvation.

My habitual procedure in the study of this subject is to examine the New Testament interpretation of the Old Testament exegetically, to consider each instance of Old Testament quotation, allusion or application in its immediate New Testament context. This procedure, I am sure, is basic and indispensable. But when it has been followed, the occasion arises to stand back at some distance and view the whole picture – in particular, to consider the dominant motifs which recur throughout the biblical literature and bind the two Testaments together. We may, for example, trace the Paradise motif from its introduction in the primaeval narrative of Genesis to the picture of Paradise Regained in the last vision of the Apocalypse. We may trace the passage from the earthly to the heavenly Jerusalem as we move from Melchizedek's city of Salem (if indeed that was Jerusalem)[3] to the New Testament portrayal of the Jerusalem that is above, metropolis of all true believers. We may trace the bread of life, the water of life, the light of life, from their earliest appearance to their utilization as symbols for the saving word of Christ in the Fourth Gospel.

Or we may consider what N. W. Porteous describes as "images which are the vehicles of the Old Testament revelation", among the more important of which he enumerates "the Election of Israel, the Covenant at Sinai-Horeb, the People of God, the Rule of God implied in the image of God as King, the Fatherhood of God, the Word of God, the Presence in the Temple, the 'Messianic' figure, the Servant of the Lord, the Son of Man."

---

[1] *Op. cit.*, p. 284.   [2] *Op. cit.*, p. 285.
[3] See pp. 70–72 below. If the picture of Jerusalem as the metropolis of the people of God (Gal. 4:26) does not go back to Melchizedek's city, it certainly goes back to David's city; cf. Ps. 87:5 (the LXX reading $\mu\acute{\eta}\tau\eta\rho\ \Sigma\iota\acute{\omega}\nu$, even if it is a misreading, sums up the sense that is in any case intended). Cf. next note.

Draw near to me, you who are untaught,
   and lodge in my school.
Why do you say you are lacking in these things,
   and why are your souls very thirsty?
I opened my mouth and said,
   "Get these things for yourselves without money.
Put your neck under the yoke,
   and let your souls receive instruction;
   it is to be found close by."[1]

Such occasional utterances of Jesus in the rôle of Divine Wisdom were probably among the factors which prompted His followers to identify Him outright with Wisdom – not only in the sense in which Paul speaks of Christ crucified as the one "whom God made our wisdom",[2] but also in the sense in which things said in the Old Testament of Wisdom, especially of Wisdom personified, are predicated of Him. His agency in creation, for example, asserted in John 1:3 f.; Col. 1:15–18 and Heb. 1:2 f.,[3] has Old Testament precedent in those passages which speak of the world as made by the word or wisdom of God,[4] and still more so when Wisdom personified speaks in the first person as the eldest daughter of God who was His close associate when creation's work began and rejoiced in all that He did.[5] This last passage is not a prophetic utterance of Christ, as so many of the Fathers thought – to the considerable embarrassment of their orthodoxy, since this interpretation represented the Uncreated Son as saying (in the Septuagint), "The Lord created me . . .".[6] But when once the identification of Christ with the Wisdom of God was established, the passage lent itself admirably (provided they could get round this embarrassment) to Christological speculation.

2. New Testament Interpretation

When G. W. Anderson was installed in the presidential chair of the (British) Society for Old Testament Study in January, 1963, he chose as the title of his inaugural lecture "Israel's Creed: Sung, not Signed".[7] This title (adapted from one of James Denney's *obiter dicta*) referred to the Psalter, considered as a synthesis of the varying ingredients in the Old

---

[1] Ben Sira's dependence in turn on Isa. 55:1 f. is plain.
[2] I Cor. 1:30.
[3] Cf. Rev. 3:14, where the title "the beginning of God's creation" is probably drawn from Prov. 8:22.
[4] E.g. Ps. 33:6; Prov. 3:19.   [5] Prov. 8:22–31.
[6] κύριος ἔκτισέν με (Prov. 8:22 LXX; cf. Sira 1:4, "Wisdom has been created [LXX ἔκτισται] before all things"). The Hebrew verb *qānāh* in Prov. 8:22 may have this sense (cf. RSV), as in Gen. 14:19, 22 (RSV "maker of heaven and earth"); but the Greek Fathers were not concerned with the Hebrew text. Athanasius counters the Arian appeal to Prov. 8:22 with the not very happy argument that it refers to the body in which the Eternal Wisdom became incarnate (*Discourse against the Arians* ii. 18–82).
[7] Published in *SJT* 16 (1963), pp. 277 ff.

deal. Here, too, the later Wisdom books, identifying Wisdom with the Torah and making a distinction between Israel and the nations,[1] differ from the earlier literature, in which there is a clearer note of universalism. It is not by chance that the hero of the book of Job is a non-Israelite, or that Arabian[2] and possibly Egyptian[3] wisdom-collections are included in the book of Proverbs.

In an article in the *Scottish Journal of Theology* for June, 1964, Walther Zimmerli relates Hebrew wisdom to the creation theme of the primaeval narrative of Genesis.[4] The God of Israel is not the God of Israel only; He is the Creator of the world, and Israel forms part of the world which He created. The world, His creation, is there to be enjoyed and explored; the study of creation reveals the greater glory of the Creator, and this is a field of knowledge open to all. True, it is possible, as Paul points out[5] – and the author of Wisdom pointed it out before him[6] – to suppress the knowledge of God which is thus accessible and to worship the creation instead of the Creator; but this is a perversion of the divine purpose. Zophar the Naamathite may ask, "Can you find out the deep things of God?"[7] but his question is not to be treated as a divine oracle imposing the answer "No". The highest function of wisdom is to guide man in this arduous quest, and wisdom's assurance, "those who seek me diligently find me"[8] anticipates our Lord's words of encouragement, "seek and you will find".[9]

This echoing by our Lord of the language of Old Testament wisdom is not unparalleled in the Gospels: indeed, some form-critics have distinguished one group of His utterances as "Wisdom sayings".[10] Where one Evangelist presents a "Q" logion as an utterance of "the Wisdom of God" – "Therefore also the Wisdom of God said, 'I will send them prophets and apostles, some of whom they will kill and persecute'..."[11] – implying perhaps a written source in some wisdom document no longer extant, another Evangelist gives it as a direct utterance of Jesus: "Therefore I send you prophets and wise men and scribes, some of whom you will kill and crucify...".[12] The *Diatessaron*, conflating the two parallel passages, makes Him say "Therefore I, the Wisdom of God, send you...". Nor can we forget that the comfortable words of Matt. 11:28–30 ("Come to me... Take my yoke upon you, and learn from me...") echo the invitation of Wisdom in Sira 51:23–26:

[1] Cf. Sira 24:23; Wisdom 12:19 ff.; Baruch 3:24–4:4.
[2] Prov. 30:1–31:9.
[3] Cf. Prov. 22:17–24:22 with the Egyptian Wisdom of Amen-em-opet.
[4] W. Zimmerli, "The Place and Limit of the Wisdom in the Framework of the Old Testament Theology", *SJT* 17 (1964), pp. 146 ff. Cf. also D. A. Hubbard, "The Wisdom Movement and Israel's Covenant Faith", *Tyndale Bulletin* 17 (1966), pp. 3 ff.
[5] Rom. 1:18 ff. [6] Wisdom 13:1 ff. [7] Job. 11:7.
[8] Prov. 8:17. [9] Matt. 7:7.
[10] Cf. R. Bultmann, *History of the Synoptic Tradition*, E.T. (Oxford, 1963), pp. 69 ff.
[11] Luke 11:49. [12] Matt. 23:34.

tian *kerygma* (or *kerygmata*) and the actual facts of the life of Jesus, in so far as they can be ascertained behind the *kerygma*. Some of Professor von Rad's pupils have made an attempt to bridge both these gulfs – in the New Testament and Old Testament alike – by showing how history and *kerygma* mutually imply each other. In the Old Testament area Rolf Rendtorff has made particularly important contributions in this respect, insisting, on the one hand, that the events of Israel's actual history, as they can be reconstructed by critical evaluation of the evidence, are integral to Old Testament theology and, on the other hand, that Israel's interpretation of the events, proclaimed in the cult and otherwise, is part of her history. We must accept both the results of historical research and Israel's confessional recital and explore more thoroughly the relation between them.[1]

Even when we try to follow the example of Professor von Rad or Professor Eichrodt, it is difficult to find one single principle around which a coherent and comprehensive Old Testament theology, doing justice to all the chief forms of Old Testament literature and teaching, can be constructed. (The same could be said about New Testament theology: when attempts are made to systematize the teaching of the New Testament, the result has often been that Paulinism has provided the framework into which the non-Pauline elements have had to be fitted, to the loss of their distinctiveness. And even "Paulinism", if that means a systematization of the teaching of the various documents in the *corpus Paulinum*, has too often involved the emphasizing of certain elements in that teaching to the disadvantage of others and a failure to do justice to the many-sided versatility of the apostle.)

For example, an approach to Old Testament theology which operates exclusively with the history of salvation as its principle finds it difficult, as Professor von Rad himself has indicated[2], to make room for the Wisdom literature. In the later Wisdom literature, indeed (the Wisdom of Ben-Sira and of pseudo-Solomon), the Old Testament *kerygma* has asserted itself: Wisdom 10:1 ff., for instance, re-tells the biblical story from Adam onwards in terms of the guidance of Wisdom, with special reference to the Exodus narrative and the wilderness wanderings. But such references are almost entirely absent from the Wisdom books of the Hebrew Bible. They may presuppose the Old Testament *kerygma*, but it plays little part in their exposition.

If we think of the covenant principle instead of the history of salvation, then, while Yahweh's covenant with Israel may be the implicit background of the canonical Wisdom books, it is not a theme with which they

---

[1] Cf. R. Rendtorff, "Geschichte und Überlieferung", in *Studien zur Theologie der alttestamentlichen Überlieferungen*, ed. R. Rendtorff and K. Koch (Neukirchen, 1961), pp. 81 ff., esp. pp. 89 ff.

[2] *Old Testament Theology* i, pp. 446, 450; he finds a similar divorce from the history of salvation in apocalyptic, which (he concludes) originated from the matrix of Wisdom (*op. cit.* ii, p. 306). Cf. also G. E. Wright, *God Who Acts* (London, 1952), pp. 103 f.

drawn by Principal Knight between the history of Israel and the history of Jesus, with special reference to the five "moments" of birth, marriage, death, resurrection and exaltation.[1] The Old Testament pattern is squeezed into the shape of the gospel story when the fall of the Judaean monarchy and consequent deportation to Babylon are said to have been "in fact, the 'crucifixion' by God himself of his own beloved Son";[2] the Old Testament pattern is imposed on the gospel story in a way that does not fit when the "moment" of marriage (which, in the former pattern, is quite properly found in the lawgiving and covenant ceremony at Sinai) is, in the latter setting, related to the proclamation of the Sermon on the Mount.[3] This is not to say that the tracing of patterns is illegitimate, but that it should not be pressed beyond the plain sense of the biblical narrative and language. It is better to think of recurring patterns of divine action and human response, along the lines indicated, for example, by H. H. Rowley[4] – all the more so because such recurring patterns were recognized by the biblical authors themselves, in both Testaments.

A break with the older organization of Old Testament theology under the heads of the doctrine of God, the doctrine of man and the doctrine of salvation (still followed in varying degrees by E. Jacob and L. Köhler), has been made in the magisterial works of W. Eichrodt and G. von Rad. Professor Eichrodt organizes the treatment of the first part of his work ("God and the People") around the covenant principle;[5] Professor von Rad finds the basis of Old Testament theology in the "history of salvation" – more precisely, in the proclamation of the mighty works of God in the Israelite cult. (This presents a sharp contrast with Köhler's exposition, in which the cult is included in the section on the doctrine of man, as though it represented man's effort to save himself.)[6]

A difficulty in Professor von Rad's presentation is the gulf existing, as he sees the situation, between the mighty acts of God celebrated in the cult and the actual facts of Israel's early history.[7] A similar gulf exists, in the mind of some New Testament theologians, between the primitive Chris-

[1] *A Christian Theology of the Old Testament*, pp. 202 ff. Since these "moments" are discerned in the Hebrew Bible only, with their Christian counterparts in the New Testament, the Apocrypha, from which they are absent, can therefore be ignored (it is argued) for purposes of biblical theology (p. 213).

[2] *Op. cit.*, p. 289.

[3] *Op. cit.*, p. 213, n. 2. Even if Jesus "preached a new Torah from the mount", as W. D. Davies says in a passage to which G. A. F. Knight refers (*Paul and Rabbinic Judaism* [London, 1948], p. 73), this analogy hardly goes far enough to warrant the recognition of the marriage theme in Matt. 5–7.

[4] H. H. Rowley, "The Authority of the Bible" in *From Moses to Qumran* (London, 1963), pp. 3 ff., esp. pp. 18 ff.

[5] Cf. the headings of the successive sections of Volume i: The Covenant Relationship, The Covenant Statutes, The Name of the Covenant God, The Nature of the Covenant God, The Instruments of the Covenant, Covenant-Breaking and Judgment, Fulfilling the Covenant.

[6] Köhler's treatment of the cult is entitled "Man's Expedient for his Own Redemption" (*Old Testament Theology*, pp. 181 ff.).

[7] Cf. G. von Rad, *Old Testament Theology* i, pp. 106 ff.

meaning in the New Testament (cf. Mt. 5:17; Lk. 24:27; Rom. 16:25-26; II Cor. 3:14-16) and in turn shed light on it and explain it.[1]

These paragraphs express eloquently the traditional Christian assessment of the Old Testament. Those who do not see the relation between the Testaments in these terms will at least concede that the New Testament presents a *sequel* to the Old – a sequel if not *the* sequel – and a story is often better appreciated in the light of its sequel.

In recent years some of the most distinguished contributions to Old Testament theology have been made from the perspective of a full biblical theology (taking both Testaments into account) by scholars who draw a clear distinction between the history of Old Testament religion (or Israel's religion) and the theology of the Old Testament. This is true not only of scholars like Wilhelm Vischer[2] and G. A. F. Knight[3] who, in the judgement of many of their colleagues, go too far in reading the New Testament back into the Old, but also of Edmond Jacob,[4] Ludwig Köhler,[5] T. C. Vriezen,[6] Walter Eichrodt[7] and Gerhard von Rad.[8]

When I mention some scholars who go too far in reading the New Testament back into the Old, I think of Professor Vischer's tendency (for all his acceptance of historical criticism) to revert to patristic precedent as when he finds in the bread and wine which Melchizedek brought for Abraham a pointer to the sacrament of the new covenant,[9] affirms that the undivulged name of the supernatural wrestler at the ford of Jabbok was Jesus Christ,[10] discerns the cross of Christ in Haman's gallows[11] or sees Christian doctrine expounded in Ecclesiastes.[12] I think too of the parallel

---

[1] English translation from *The Documents of Vatican II*, ed. W. M. Abbott and J. Gallagher (London, 1966). Grateful acknowledgement is hereby made of the courtesy of the publishers in granting permission to quote these three paragraphs (see Preface.)
[2] W. Vischer, *Das Christuszeugnis des Alten Testaments* i (Zurich, ⁶1943), ii. 1 (Zurich, 1942); E. T. *The Witness of the Old Testament to Christ* i (London, 1949).
[3] G. A. F. Knight, *A Christian Theology of the Old Testament* (London, 1959).
[4] E. Jacob, *Théologie de l'Ancien Testament* (Neuchatel and Paris, 1955); E. T., *Theology of the Old Testament* (London, 1958).
[5] L. Köhler, *Theologie des Alten Testaments* (Tübingen, ³1953); E. T., *Old Testament Theology* (London, 1957).
[6] T. C. Vriezen, *Hoofdlijnen der Theologie van het Oude Testament* (Wageningen, ²1954); E. T., *An Outline of Old Testament Theology* (Wageningen, 1958).
[7] W. Eichrodt, *Theologie des Alten Testaments* i (Stuttgart, ⁶1959), ii/iii (Stuttgart, ⁵1964); E. T., *Theology of the Old Testament* i (London, 1961), ii (London, 1967).
[8] G. von Rad, *Theologie des Alten Testaments* i (Munich, 1957), ii (Munich, 1960); E. T., *Old Testament Theology* i (Edinburgh, 1962), ii (Edinburgh, 1965). An interesting survey is provided in W. McKane's inaugural lecture as Professor of Hebrew and Oriental Languages in the University of St. Andrews, "Modern Trends in Old Testament Theology" (*St. Mary's College Bulletin*, 10, Spring 1968, pp. 7 ff.).
[9] *Das Christuszeugnis des Alten Testaments*⁶, i, p. 164. This is, remarkably, the one outstanding feature in the Melchizedek narrative of Gen. 14:18 ff. which is passed over without mention in Heb. 7:1 ff.
[10] *Op. cit.*, p. 189.
[11] "The Book of Esther", *EQ* 11 (1939), pp. 3 ff., esp. pp. 11 ff.
[12] *Der Prediger Salomo* (Munich, 1926).

the use made of the Exodus motif to depict the return from the Babylonian exile and the use made of the same motif to depict the New Testament message of salvation.[1] Historic Christianity recognizes in the New Testament the goal or *telos* of the Old, and we do not need to go all the way with Aristotle to agree with him that anything is better understood in the light of its *telos*.

One of the most recent examples of this recognition is provided by Chapter IV of the *Constitution on Divine Revelation* adopted by Vatican Council II. Chapter IV is entitled "Concerning the Old Testament", and I take leave to quote three of its paragraphs which are of particular relevance:

> 14. In carefully planning and preparing the salvation of the whole human race, the God of supreme love, by a special dispensation, chose for Himself a people to whom He might entrust His promises. First He entered into a covenant with Abraham (cf. Gen. 15:18) and, through Moses, with the people of Israel (cf. Ex. 24:8). To this people which He had acquired for Himself, He so manifested Himself through words and deeds as the one true and living God that Israel came to know by experience the ways of God with men, and with God Himself speaking to them through the mouth of the prophets, Israel daily gained a deeper and clearer understanding of His ways and made them more widely known among the nations (cf. Ps. 21:28-29; 95:1-3; Is. 2:1-4; Jer. 3:17). The plan of salvation, foretold by the sacred authors, recounted and explained by them, is found as the true word of God in the books of the Old Testament: these books, therefore, written under divine inspiration, remain permanently valuable. "For whatever things have been written have been written for our instruction, that through the patience and the consolation afforded by the Scriptures we may have hope" (Rom. 15:4).
>
> 15. The principal purpose to which the plan of the Old Covenant was directed was to prepare for the coming both of Christ, the universal Redeemer, and of the messianic kingdom, to announce this coming by prophecy (cf. Lk. 24:44; Jn. 5:39; I Pet. 1:10), and to indicate its meaning through various types (cf. I Cor. 10:11). Now the books of the Old Testament, in accordance with the state of mankind before the time of salvation established by Christ, reveal to all men the knowledge of God and of man and the ways in which God, just and merciful, deals with men. These books, though they also contain some things which are incomplete and temporary, nevertheless show us true divine pedagogy. These same books, then, give expression to a lively sense of God, contain a store of sublime teachings about God, sound wisdom about human life, and a wonderful treasury of prayers, and in them the mystery of our salvation is present in a hidden way. Christians should receive them with reverence.
>
> 16. God, the inspirer and author of both Testaments, wisely arranged that the New Testament be hidden in the Old and the Old be made manifest in the New. For, though Christ established the New Covenant in His blood (cf. Lk. 22:20; I Cor. 11:25), still the books of the Old Testament with all their parts, caught up into the proclamation of the gospel, acquire and show forth their full

---

[1] See pp. 33 ff., 47 ff.

CHAPTER I

ORGANIZING OLD TESTAMENT THEOLOGY

"To him all the prophets bear witness."

THE PAYTON LECTURES, IT IS PRESCRIBED, "MUST FALL WITHIN THESE areas: the uniqueness or confirmation of the historic Christian faith, the confutation of non-Christian or sub-Christian views, or the foundation of Biblical doctrines". The last of these categories, it seems to me, is the one under which my particular subject can most properly fall. It was in this very area of study that the doyen of British New Testament scholars, Professor C. H. Dodd, in another series of lectures delivered in the United States, found "the sub-structure of Christian theology".[1] It would be a fruitless enterprise indeed to traverse the ground covered by Professor Dodd, in hope of finding something which he overlooked, but the following treatment of the relation between the Testaments proceeds along different lines from his.

1. Old Testament Theology

One of my colleagues in the University of Manchester a few years ago, discussing the question "Is there an Old Testament Theology?" made the statement that

> the use of the Old Testament in the New is the concern of the New Testament scholar, and not of the Old Testament scholar; the latter should not go to the New Testament except in isolated instances for the purpose of textual criticism and should never for a moment forget that, so far as he is concerned, it is the original meaning of the text that matters, and not the use which was later made of it in the New Testament.[2]

There is a valid point there, although it could be argued that the history of Old Testament interpretation is a proper field of study for the Old Testament scholar; but as a New Testament student I gladly avail myself of the permission thus granted me to read the Old Testament in the light of the New. There is something more to be said: if we begin to atomize the Christian scriptures we cannot treat even the Old Testament by itself as a unity or Old Testament theology as a single subject of study. The Old Testament is interpreted in the New, it is true, but the Old Testament is also interpreted in the Old. There is, for example, a relation between

---
[1] The sub-title of C. H. Dodd, *According to the Scriptures* (London, 1952), the Stone Lectures delivered at Princeton Theological Seminary in 1950.
[2] P. Wernberg-Møller, *Hibbert Journal* 59 (1960–61), pp. 21 ff., esp. p. 29.

PREFACE

"This is that which was spoken by the prophet."

WHEN I WAS HONOURED WITH AN INVITATION TO DELIVER THE Payton Lectures for 1968 in Fuller Theological Seminary, Pasadena, California, President D. A. Hubbard informed me that the topic suggested by the Faculty was "The Relationship of the Old Testament to the New" and encouraged me to develop this topic along the lines of my own approach. This I have endeavoured to do, by selecting a few Old Testament themes which are taken over in the New Testament as vehicles for expressing, in a diversity of ways, the Christian paradox that the crucified Jesus is universal Lord.

Only part of the following material was actually delivered during the four lecture periods, but the lecturing style has been preserved throughout.

It is at once a duty and a delight to place on record my gratitude to the President, the Dean, the Faculty and the student body of Fuller Theological Seminary, whose kindness has made my visit to Pasadena a very pleasant memory, and not least to my old friends Geoffrey and Isobel Bromiley who entertained me in their home for the week of the lectures. The work of preparing the lectures for publication has been greatly lightened for me by the efficient and willing assistance of my secretary, Miss Margaret Hogg.

Excerpts from The Constitution on Divine Revelation (pp. 12 f.) are taken from *The Documents of Vatican II*, published by Guild Press, America Press, Association Press, and Herder and Herder, and copyrighted 1966 by the America Press; and are used by permission.

July 1968   F.F.B.

CONTENTS

		page
	Preface	9
I.	Organizing Old Testament Theology	11
II.	The Rule of God	22
III.	The Salvation of God	32
IV.	The Victory of God	40
V.	The People of God	51
VI.	The Son of David	68
VII.	The Servant Messiah	83
VIII.	The Shepherd King	100
	Abbreviations	115
	Index	117

VIRO REVERENDO
DAVID ALLAN HUBBARD
SCHOLAE FULLERIANAE
IN OPPIDO PASADENA
PRAESIDI
CONLEGISQVE EIVS
SS THEOLOGIAE PROFESSORIBVS
GRATO ANIMO
D.D.D.
AVCTOR

Copyright © 1968 The Paternoster Press

This American Edition is published by arrangement with
The Paternoster Press, Exeter, England

Made and Printed in Great Britain

THE NEW TESTAMENT DEVELOPMENT OF OLD TESTAMENT THEMES

by

F. F. BRUCE

M.A. *(Cantab.)*, D.D. *(Aberd.)*

*Rylands Professor of Biblical Criticism and Exegesis
in the University of Manchester*

"This is that which was spoken by the prophet" (Acts 2: 16)

Wm. B. Eerdmans Publishing Company
Grand Rapids, Michigan

Other works by F. F. Bruce:

THE SPREADING FLAME
ISRAEL AND THE NATIONS
AN EXPANDED PARAPHRASE OF THE EPISTLES OF PAUL
SECOND THOUGHTS ON THE DEAD SEA SCROLLS
THE TEACHER OF RIGHTEOUSNESS IN THE QUMRAN TEXTS
BIBLICAL EXEGESIS IN THE QUMRAN TEXTS
THE ACTS OF THE APOSTLES: GREEK TEXT WITH INTRODUCTION AND COMMENTARY
THE BOOK OF THE ACTS: ENGLISH TEXT WITH EXPOSITION AND NOTES
THE EPISTLE TO THE HEBREWS: ENGLISH TEXT WITH EXPOSITION AND NOTES
THE EPISTLE TO THE COLOSSIANS: ENGLISH TEXT WITH EXPOSITION AND NOTES
THE EPISTLE TO THE EPHESIANS: A VERSE-BY-VERSE EXPOSITION
THE EPISTLE OF PAUL TO THE ROMANS: AN INTRODUCTION AND COMMENTARY
PAUL AND HIS CONVERTS
THE NEW TESTAMENT DOCUMENTS: ARE THEY RELIABLE?
THE APOSTOLIC DEFENCE OF THE GOSPEL
THE BOOKS AND THE PARCHMENTS
THE ENGLISH BIBLE
THE HITTITES AND THE OLD TESTAMENT

THE NEW TESTAMENT DEVELOPMENT
OF OLD TESTAMENT THEMES

INDEX

Aaron, 56
Abbott, W. M., 13
Abomination of desolation, 108
Abraham, 13, 32 f., 51 ff., 61, 68
Abrahams, I., 110
Acts of the Apostles, 37
Agamemnon, 100
Ahab, 102
Akeldama (Field of Blood), 109, 110
Albright, W. F., 44
Amos, 24, 58, 60, 72, 76, 79
Ancient of Days, 26, 81
Anderson, G. W., 17 f.
Antioch (Pisidian), 37, 69, 78, 87
Antiochus IV (Epiphanes), 90, 91, 99
Apocalypse, 31, 44, 50, 61, 64, 74, 79, 96, 111
Aquila (translator), 98
Asherah, 41
Assyria, Assyrians, 30, 43, 58, 65, 66, 72, 73
Athanasius, 17
Atonement, Day of, 94

Baal, 41, 42, 43, 57
Babylon, Babylonians, 32 f., 43, 47, 48, 73
Balaam, 30, 76, 79
Baptism, 62 f., 85
Barrett, C. K., 99
Bauer, W., 107
Bethlehem, 73, 77, 78
Black, M., 30, 97
Booths (Tabernacles), Feast of, 23 f., 44 f., 108
Bornkamm, G., 50
Borsch, F. H., 26, 97
"Branch", 74, 76
Brownlee, W. H., 89, 94
Bruce, F. F., 36, 49, 91, 103
Bultmann, R., 16, 21

Caesarea Philippi, 81
Chronicler, 111
Codrus, 30
Conzelmann, H., 38
Corinth, 93
Covenant, 14, 18, 21, 46, 51 ff., 69, 70, 90, 99, 102
Cowper, W., 41
Cullmann, O., 21, 38
Cyril of Jerusalem, 63
Cyrus, 83 ff.

Daniel, 26 f., 29, 66, 75, 81, 90, 98, 99
David (king), 18, 25, 26, 37, 50, 68, 78 ff., 83, 89, 90, 97, 100 f., 107, 110, 111, 112
Davies, W. D., 14
Day of the Lord, 24, 44 f., 107 f.
Decius Mus, P., 30
Del Medico, H. E., 110
Denney, J., 17
Dentan, R. C., 101
Deuteronomy, 34, 35, 36 f., 67
Diatessaron, 16
Dodd, C. H., 11, 31, 66, 97, 101, 108, 109
Dosa (rabbi), 112
Dragon, 41 ff., 48
Duhm, B., 111

Eaton, J. H., 44
Egypt, 23, 34, 42, 43, 100
Eichrodt, W., 13, 14, 15
Eissfeldt, O., 101, 111
Eleazar ben Qalir, 94
Election, 18, 59 ff., 65, 84, 86
Elijah, 57 ff.
Elisha, 75
Ellis, E. E., 38
Engnell, I., 89
Enoch, Similitudes of, 27, 91 f.

INDEX

Entry into Jerusalem, 106
Ephesians (epistle), 62, 64
Ethiopian chancellor, 89, 94
Exodus, 19, 23, 32 ff., 42, 43, 45 ff., 49, 110
Ezekiel, 33, 54 f., 72, 73, 74, 76, 89, 101, 111, 112
Ezra, 33

Farrer, A. M., 50
Flender, H., 39
"Flock", 104, 106
France, R. T., 97
Fuller, D. P., 39
Fuller, R. H., 28

Gallagher, J., 13
Genesis, 41, 51, 61
Gideon, 25
Glory (Presence), 18, 19, 20, 30
Gordon, C. H., 103
Guilding, A., 103, 110
Gundry, R. H., 109

Habakkuk, 37 f., 44 f.
Hadad-rimmon, 111, 113
Haggai, 74
Haman, 13
Hanson, A. T., 35
Ḥasidim, 27, 57, 99
Hasmonaeans, 76, 101
Hebert, A. G., 68
Hebrews (epistle), 33, 35, 53, 55 ff., 64, 79, 96
Higgins, A. J. B., 28, 97, 99
Hooke, S. H., 19, 32, 65, 89
Hooker, M. D., 27, 28, 29, 97, 99
Hophra (Pharaoh), 43
Hosea, 63, 64, 66 f., 72
Hubbard, D. A., 17
Hvidberg, F. F., 112

Isaiah, 30, 59, 65, 66, 72 f., 76, 103
Isaiah (chapters 40–55), 33, 47 ff., 69 ff., 83 ff., 106

Jacob (blessing of), 73 f., 76
Jacob, E., 13, 14

James the Just, 79
Jehoiachin (Jeconiah), 74, 78, 89
Jephthah's daughter, 111
Jeremiah, 53, 54, 56, 72, 73, 74, 88, 89, 108 f.
Jeremias, J., 96, 100
Jerome, 63
Jerusalem (*see also* Zion), 18 f., 71, 79, 88, 107, 108, 111
Jeshua (high priest), 74, 75
Jesse, 76, 90
Job, 41 f.
John (Baptist), 38, 88
John (Evangelist), 30 f., 96, 104, 107, 108, 110, 112 f.
Johnson, A. R., 22, 45, 46
Joshua, 36
Joshua ben Levi (rabbi), 107
Josiah, 111
Judah (tribe), 68, 73 f.
Judas (Iscariot), 108 ff.
Jude (epistle), 35 f.
Justin, 31, 63

King (of Israel), 25, 30 f., 46, 48 f., 68 ff., 89 f., 100 ff., 102, 112, 113
Kittim, 30, 76
Knight, G. A. F., 13, 14
Knox, W. L., 41
Koch, K., 15
Köhler, L., 13, 14
Kuhn, H. W., 107

Lamarche, P., 103, 112, 113
"Lamb", 50, 79, 96, 110, 112 f.
Leeuw, V. de, 90
Leprosy, 89, 94
Levi (tribe), 72, 76
Leviathan, 42, 43, 44
Lindars, B., 98
Loewe, H., 93
Lohse, E., 38
Luke, 38 f., 51 ff., 77, 78, 85, 86, 94, 95, 99, 107

Macaulay, T. B., 27
Maccabees, 29
McKane, W., 13

INDEX

Mackay, C., 108
Malachi, 101
Manson, T. W., 95, 104
Manson, W., 108
Marduk, 41
Mark, 95, 102 ff., 107, 109
Martin, R. P., 63
Mary, 51, 77
Maśkilim, 90 f., 99
Massoretic text, 106, 111
Matthew, 106 f., 108 ff.
Mauchline, J., 43
Megiddo, 111, 113
Melchizedek, 13, 18, 56, 71, 79
Meshullam, 89
Messiah (ben David), 18, 50, 74 ff., 80, 81, 83 ff., 90, 93, 94, 107, 112
Messiah (ben Joseph), 112
Micah, 72, 73, 100 f., 103
Micaiah ben Imlah, 102, 104
Michel, O., 107
Moore, T. V., 114
Moses, 36, 49, 53 ff., 64, 67, 89, 100 f.
Mowinckel, S., 26

Nathan, 70, 76
Nazareth, 85
Nebuchadnezzar, 26, 66, 89
North, C. R., 90

Olives, Mount of, 95, 108
Onias III, 75, 111
Origen, 29
Otzen, B., 101, 102, 105

Paradise, 18
Passover, 23, 34, 49, 96, 110, 112 f.
Paul, 31, 33, 34, 35, 37, 38, 49, 52 ff., 57 ff., 62, 64, 69, 78, 93, 95, 99
Paulinism, 15
Pentateuch, 51
People of God, 18, 21, 51 ff., 63
Perdelwitz, R., 63
Peshitta, 110
Peter (apostle), 85, 94, 98, 109
Peter (first epistle), 62 ff., 96
Philistines, 71
"Pierced One", 110 ff.

Pilate, 30 f.
Porteous, N. W., 18 f.
Priest, Priesthood, 56, 64, 72, 73, 76, 89
Priest-King, 64
Prophet, Prophecy, 21, 49, 72, 89
Psalms (canonical), 17 f., 37, 42, 43, 44, 63, 65, 70, 75, 100, 109, 113
Psalms of Solomon, 52, 76 f.
Pseudo-Philo, 35
Pusey, E. B., 114

Qumran, 29, 49, 74, 76, 91, 92, 93, 94, 97, 98, 99, 101, 104, 108, 110, 114

Rabin, Ch., 103
Rad, G. von, 13, 14, 15, 36, 68
Rahab, 41, 43, 48
Rashi, 112
Reinach, T., 110
"Remnant", 57 ff.
Rendtorff, R., 15
Robinson, T. H., 44
Romans, 76 f.
Rowley, H. H., 14, 44, 59, 90, 99
Rule of God, 18, 21, 22 ff.

Sacrifices, 14, 64
Salvation, history of, 14, 18, 21, 32 ff., 40 ff.
Samuel, 25
Schweizer, E., 28
Sea, 22 f., 42, 43, 44, 45, 46, 49
Seleucids, 30
Sellin, E., 111
Septuagint, 17, 18, 79, 81, 93, 96, 98, 100, 106
Servant of the Lord, 18, 21, 29, 30, 61, 78, 80, 82, 83 ff., 103, 112
Sharman, H. B., 27
Shekinah (*see also* Glory), 30
"Shepherd", 74, 80, 100 ff.
Sheshbazzar, 74
Silver (thirty pieces), 105, 108 f.
Simeon (of Jerusalem), 86
Simon (Hasmonaean), 111
Sinai, 53 f.
Smith, G. A., 59
Snaith, N. H., 47

INDEX

Solomon, 72, 78, 79
Solomon, Odes of, 44
Son of David, 21, 68 ff., 97
Son of Man, 18, 21, 26 ff., 61, 81, 97 f.
Sperber, A., 93
"Star", 79
Stenning, J. F., 93
Stephen, 28, 33, 36
"Stone", 63, 65 f.
Streeter, B. H., 63
Symmachus, 98

Talmud, 94, 107, 112
Tammuz, 89, 111
Targum, 93, 113
Teacher of Righteousness, 92, 97, 103
Temple, 64, 79, 105, 109, 113
Testaments of Twelve Patriarchs, 76
Theodotion, 98
Tiamat, 41
Tödt, H. E., 28, 97
Traders, 106, 113

Ugarit, 41, 43, 44, 103
Uzziah, 89

Vatican Council II, 12
Vielhauer, P., 28

Vineyard (parable), 66
Virgin oracle, 73, 103
Vischer, W., 13
Vos, G., 55, 75
Vriezen, T. C., 13, 59

Wernberg-Møller, P., 11
Wesley, C., 25, 40 f.
Westcott, B. F., 56 f.
Westermann, C., 21
Wicked Priest, 91
Wilson, J. A., 100
Wisdom, 15 ff., 60
"Word", 18, 19 f.
Wright, G. E., 15, 37

Young, E. J., 89

Zadok, 72, 76
Zadokite Work, 103 f., 106
Zechariah (book of), 49, 74, 75, 101 ff.
Zechariah (priest), 51, 77
Zedekiah, 73, 89
Zerubbabel, 74, 75, 76, 89
Zimmerli, W., 16
Zion (see also Jerusalem), 22, 48, 65, 68, 70, 75, 84, 106, 109